SEW YOUR OWN
SOFT FURNISHINGS

40 BEAUTIFUL TABLE & BED LINENS TO MAKE YOURSELF

DOROTHY WOOD

southwater

This edition is published by Southwater, an imprint of Anness Publishing Ltd, Hermes House, 88–89 Blackfriars Road, London SE1 8HA; tel. 020 7401 2077; fax 020 7633 9499

www.southwaterbooks.com; www.annesspublishing.com

If you like the images in this book and would like to investigate using them for publishing, promotions or advertising, please visit our website www.practicalpictures.com for more information.

UK distributor: Book Trade Services; tel. 0116 2759086; fax 0116 2759090; uksales@booktradeservices.com; exportsales@booktradeservices.com
North American distributor: National Book Network; tel. 301 459 3366; fax 301 429 5746; www.nbnbooks.com
Australian distributor: Pan Macmillan Australia; tel. 1300 135 113; fax 1300 135 103; customer.service@macmillan.com.au
New Zealand distributor: David Bateman Ltd; tel. (09) 415 7664; fax (09) 415 8892

ETHICAL TRADING POLICY

At Anness Publishing we believe that business should be conducted in an ethical and ecologically sustainable way, with respect for the environment and a proper regard to the replacement of the natural resources we employ. We are therefore currently growing more than 750,000 trees in three Scottish forest plantations. These forests contain more than 3.5 times the number of trees employed each year in making paper for the books we manufacture.
Because of this ongoing ecological investment programme, you, as our customer, can have the pleasure and reassurance of knowing that a tree is being cultivated on your behalf to naturally replace the materials used to make the book you are holding.
For further information, go to www.annesspublishing.com/trees

A CIP catalogue record for this book is available from the British Library.

Previously published as *Making Table & Bed-Linen*

Publisher **Joanna Lorenz**
Editorial Director **Helen Sudell**
Project Editor **Simona Hill**
Photographer **Paul Bricknell**
Step-by-step Photographer **Rodney Forte**
Stylist **Juliana Leite Goad**
Designer **Lisa Tai**
Editorial Reader **Kate Humby**
Production Controller **Don Campaniello**

The publishers would like to thank the following organizations and individuals who generously loaned images for inclusion in this book:
Lucienne Linen p8 below and p10 top.
Nordic Style p9, p11.
IPC Magazines, p9 left, Tim Evan Cook.

All projects were made by the author, except the following: Penny Mayor made the corner pleat dining chair cover, the simple chair cover, napkin and a tablecloth. Beryl Miller made the scallop-edge chair and pleated chair back. Kath Poxon made the cot (crib) quilt. Lucinda Ganderton made the appliqué blanket. Penny Boylan made the pillowcase edgings. Rita Whitehorn made the bed quilt. Sally Burton made the beaded tablerunner, placemat, and a tablecloth.

PUBLISHER'S NOTE

Although the advice and information in this book are believed to be accurate and true at the time of going to press, neither the authors nor the publisher can accept any legal responsibility or liability for any errors or omissions that may have been made nor for any inaccuracies nor for any loss, harm or injury that comes about from following instructions or advice in this book.

SEW YOUR OWN
SOFT FURNISHINGS

contents

introduction

Bed linen and table

linen are practical soft

furnishings that can be

kept purely functional,

or can be made into

something really special

using good-quality

fabrics and interesting

decorative details. Start

with basic projects such

as a tied-edge

pillowcase or tablecloth

then move on to more

challenging projects.

bed linen

Bedrooms are very personal rooms that are not normally seen by anyone other than family members or overnight guests. As a result, the bedroom is a place where you can indulge personal preferences and make it as pretty or striking as you like. Nowadays the majority of people choose streamlined duvet covers with a fitted sheet underneath, but there is always call for a traditional bedcover, either to provide extra warmth and comfort in the winter or with a flat sheet for a cool alternative in the summer. Patchwork quilts are always appealing and we have included one here that can be made quickly on a sewing machine using large patches of fabric and a selection of fabrics and colours.

left above The classic blue and white often associated with sea and sand does not need to mean bold deckchair stripes. Here a plain blue and white duvet cover is complemented with a beautiful Oxford pillowcase with a sheer fabric flange.

left below White-on-white embroidery is timeless and adds a subtle decorative touch to bed linen. For pillowcases to be used for sleeping, keep the decoration to the outside edge.

right This unashamedly feminine room has a delicate floral patterned quilt, softened by the delightful scalloped edge.

There is a great deal of soft furnishing in a bedroom but much of it is actually on the bed, which takes up most of the space in the majority of bedrooms. The bed linen should therefore be central to any scheme. As well as a duvet or bedcover, the majority of beds have a valance (dust ruffle) – that's the deep panel of fabric that hangs over the edge of the bed base and covers the legs of the bed attractively. Valances can either be made in the same fabric as the bed linen or they can be more formal and be made in furnishing fabric to match the upholstery or curtains in the room. Lightweight fabrics can be gathered or pleated but heavier fabrics hang better if flat with a simple pleat at each corner.

Pillows are an essential in any bedroom. These can be standard rectangles, usually hidden under the duvet, or the more luxurious square pillows that look quite stunning propped at an angle at the top of the bed. These large pillows help to break up the expanse of the duvet or bedcover, and do not need to be used for sleeping – they can be tossed on a chair overnight. As a result such pillowcases can be quite decorative, with lace edging or some beautiful embroidery on the front.

Although the majority of us have duvets there is still a place for the bedcover. A patchwork quilt, for example, will look quite stunning and keep the dust off a made-up bed in the spare room. Alternatively it can be used with a sheet as a cool alternative to a duvet in the summer and a simple throw can add an extra layer of warmth to the duvet in the winter.

Whatever arrangement you decide to have, all bed linen has to be practical, as it needs to be changed and laundered regularly. For the most part this means cotton or cotton/polyester mixes. The advantage of cotton or cotton-mix fabrics is that many are sold in sheeting widths, wide enough even for a king-sized bed. You can be quite inventive and add a linen border to the edge of cotton sheets and pillowcases, or use it for an envelope opening on a duvet cover. More unusual fabrics can be used for bed linen, but you must ensure that the fabric is comfortable against the skin. A throw can be made from a warm fleece fabric, but the edge should be bound in linen or cotton so that it is comfortable to tuck under your chin. Textured fabrics make wonderful outer bedcovers – you can use these fabrics for the top layer of a duvet and put a plain fabric on the underside and as a border along the top edge so that it is more comfortable to use.

There are many styles of bed, and some, such as four-poster beds, look much better with drapes of some sort. Bed drapes can be simply a length of fabric that hangs

over bars above the bed to form a canopy or tent. The style of canopy can instantly transform a bedroom, creating a minimalist look; an exotic, ethnic room with rich fabrics, tassels and deep fringing; or something much more romantic with plenty of lace and large luxurious bows.

There are plenty of inspiring pictures to help you create the perfect bedroom, and clear step-by-step instructions for making everything from a basic pillowcase to a stunning corona or bed drape in beautiful or exotic fabrics. There are easy projects for the novice stitcher and clear instructions to allow anyone to build on skills so that they can achieve any of the ideas in the book. This section finishes with pretty ideas to furnish a new nursery.

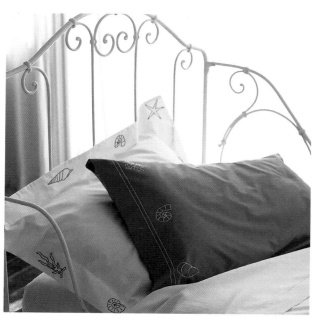

far left *Toile de jouy* fabric is used to co-ordinate bed linen with other soft furnishings in the room.

top left Plain white bed linen can be transformed with beautiful embroidery. Here single rose motifs have been used alongside pretty garlands to make a complete set.

below left Plain pillowcases can be personalized with simple motifs. For comfort, keep the embroidery away from the centre where your face touches the pillow.

right Mixed check fabrics can be made into a simple quilt in a weekend to make a very practical bedcover for a child's room.

standard bed and cot sizes

Bed sizes vary considerably between countries, but as a guide the following were used for the projects.

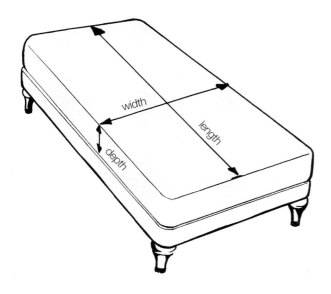

Single bed	90 x 190cm/3 x 6½ft
Small double bed	135 x 190cm/4½ x 6½ft
Standard double bed	150 x 200cm/5 x 6½ft
King-size bed	180 x 200cm/6 x 6½ft
Standard cot	56 x 118cm/22 x 46in
Continental cot	60 x 120cm/24 x 47in
Extra-large cot	63 x 127cm/25 x 50in
Cot bed	70 x 140cm/27½ x 55in

basic pillowcase

The basic pillowcase is made from a single strip of fabric that is simply hemmed, folded and stitched down both sides. The pillow is tucked under the flap on the inside to hold it firmly and neatly in place. The basic pillowcase can be made in the same colour as the sheet or as a contrast and can be decorated with ribbon, embroidery or appliqué.

calculating the fabric

The length of the fabric is double the length of the pillow with 20cm/ 8in added for hem and flap allowance. The width of the fabric is the width of the pillow with 3cm/1¼in seam allowance added.

you will need

- **pillow**
- **fabric**
- **sewing kit**

tip for basic pillowcase
Add ribbon or other trimmings before you stitch the side seams.

1 Press and stitch a double 5mm/¼in hem at one short end of the fabric and a double 2cm/¾in hem at the other end.

2 Fold the narrower hem end over to make a 15cm/6in flap with the right side facing out. Pin across the hem.

3 Fold the pillowcase in half crossways with wrong sides together. Pin and stitch a 5mm/ ¼in seam down both sides.

4 Press the seam open and turn through. Stitch an 8mm/⅜in French seam (see basic techniques).

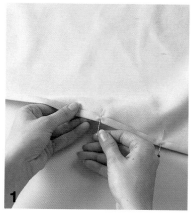

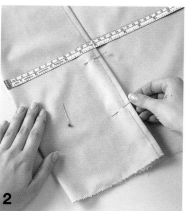

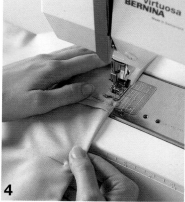

pillowcase with a border

This pretty pillowcase is simply the basic pillowcase with a decorative contrast border added before the pillowcase is made up. Narrow piping can be added between the border and the main pillowcase or the border can be embroidered by hand or machine.

calculating the fabric

The width of both fabrics is the width of the pillow with 3cm/1¼in seam allowance added. The length of the main fabric is 10cm/4in less than double the length of the pillow. The depth of the contrast border fabric is 33cm/13in.

you will need

- **pillow**
- **main fabric**
- **contrast fabric**
- **sewing kit**

tip for pillowcase with a border
Using flat fell and French seams hides any raw edges and makes the pillowcase harder wearing.

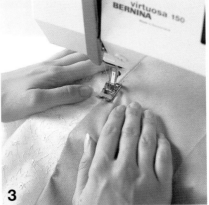

1 Press and stitch a 2cm/¾in double hem on one short edge of the main fabric and make a 5mm/¼in double hem on one longer edge of the contrast fabric.

2 Pin the raw edges of the two pieces right sides together and stitch a 1.5cm/⅝in seam. Press the seam towards the darker fabric. Trim the underneath seam allowance to 5mm/¼in.

3 Turn the other edge of the seam allowance under and press to prepare a flat fell seam (see basic techniques). Stitch the edge of the seam or use one of the decorative embroidery stitches on the machine. Complete this pillowcase as a basic pillowcase making a 15cm/6in flap on the contrast fabric and stitching the sides with French seams.

buttoned pillowcase

Buttons make an attractive addition to a pillowcase but as they are hard and uncomfortable to lean against, must be kept well away from where your head might lie. To solve this problem, add an attractive border to the outside edge of the pillowcase.

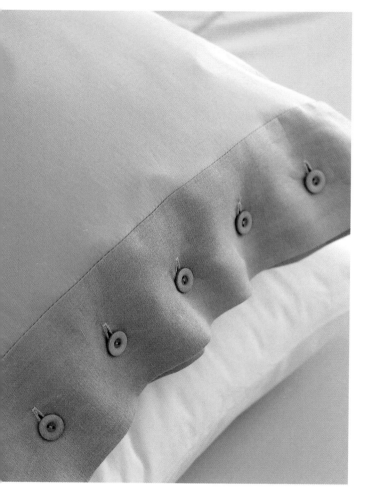

calculating the fabric

Cut the main fabric for the pillowcase the length and width of the pillow, adding 3cm/1¼in seam allowance to each measurement. Cut two pieces for the button border 23cm/9in long and the same width as the main fabric.

you will need

- **pillow**
- **main fabric**
- **contrast fabric**
- **buttons**
- **sewing kit**

tip for buttoned pillowcase

If you can't find buttons to match, cover buttons in a contrast fabric.

1 With right sides together, join the side seams of the border panels with 1.5cm/⅝in flat seams. Press open. Fold the main fabric in half and stitch together along the long edges.

2 Turn the pillowcase right side out. Place the border on top with right sides together. Match the side seams and pin, then stitch around the top edge. Press the seam towards the border.

3 Turn in a 1.5cm/⅝in hem on the raw edge of the border. Fold over the edge of the border to meet the stitching on the inside. Pin and tack (baste) in position. Hem the border to the stitching.

4 Insert pins along the centre of the border. Measure and mark the buttonholes with tacking thread.

5 Make machine buttonholes on the top of the border using a toning thread. With sharp, pointed scissors, slit the buttonholes. Sew the buttons in the corresponding position on the inside back edge of the border. Stitch over a pin to create a shank behind the button (see basic techniques).

tied-edge pillowcase

Ties add an unusual touch to a simple pillowcase design. Vary the look by making the ties wide or narrow and alter the length so that they will tie into a simple knot or make a pretty bow. You could make ties from contrasting fabric or ribbon.

calculating the fabric

Add 3cm/1¼in to the width of the pillow and 23cm/9in to double the length of the pillow.

For the ties shown here you will need 40 x 50cm/16 x 20in of fabric.

you will need

- pillow
- main fabric
- sewing kit

tip for tied-edge pillowcase
For an alternative look use a contrast pillowcase over the pillow.

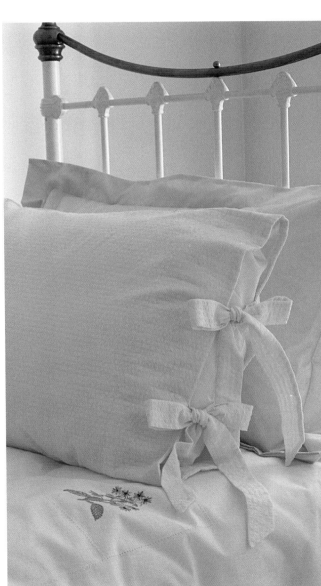

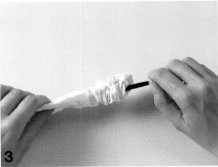

1 Cut four ties each 10 x 50cm/4 x 20in lengthways down the fabric. Fold the main fabric in half and stitch the sides with French seams (see basic techniques). Cut off the top 10cm/4in and put to one side for the facing.

2 Fold the ties in half lengthways with right sides together. Stitch down the long side and diagonally across one short end with a 1.5cm/½in seam. Trim the point to reduce bulk.

3 Turn the tie through. Ease out the point and press flat.

4 Tack two ties equal distances from the centre point on one side of the pillowcase with raw edges aligned. Match the ties on the other side. Pin the facing over the ties with right sides together. Match the seams and stitch.

5 To finish, turn a small hem on the raw edge of the facing and stitch the hem in place.

Oxford pillowcase

An Oxford pillowcase has a flat border all the way round that makes the pillow look fuller and more substantial. The border can be added in a contrast fabric but this simple method looks quite stunning made in a sheer fabric with a contrast basic pillowcase inside.

calculating the fabric

Cut the width of each piece 13cm/5in wider than the pillow. The front panel is 13cm/5in longer than the pillow. The back panel is 10cm/4in longer than the pillow and the flap is 30cm/12in deep.

you will need

• pillow
• organza
• sewing kit

tip for Oxford pillowcase

If you find sheer fabric difficult to stitch on your machine, cut strips of tissue paper and stitch through the paper to complete the seams. Tear off the paper.

1 Pull a thread and cut along the gathers to ensure the fabric is cut straight. Cut all three pieces from the fabric with the lengthways straight grain running down the pillow.

2 Pin and tack (baste) a 2cm/¾in double hem along one short edge of the back panel and along a long edge of the flap. Stitch each hem close to the fold.

3 Place the hemmed flap panel on top of the front panel with the wrong sides together and pin. Arrange the back panel on top and tack all the way around.

4 Stitch a 9mm/⅜in seam and trim to 3mm/⅛in. Trim across the corners. Press the seams open as far into the corners as possible.

5 Turn the pillowcase through and roll the edge between your fingers. Tack the edge to hold the fabric flat.

6 Measure 5cm/2in from the needle and stick a piece of masking tape on to the sewing machine to mark the distance. Top-stitch the border using the tape as a guide.

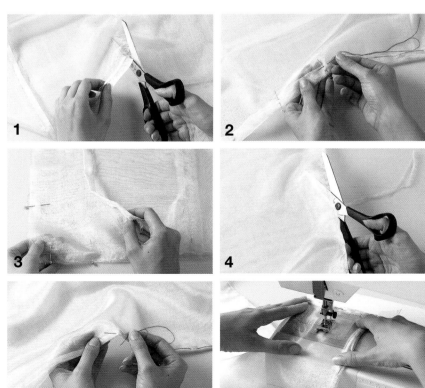

ruffled pillowcase

The ruffle is made of the same fabric as the body of the pillow, but it could be made from a contrast colour or fabric type. The ruffle can be decorated with ribbon or lace before gathering. The pillow can be embroidered with a monogram or embroidery.

calculating the fabric

Cut the width of each piece 3cm/1¼in wider than the pillow. The front panel is 3cm/1¼in longer than the pillow. The back panel is 5.5cm/2¼in longer than the pillow and the flap is 25cm/10in deep. The length of the ruffle is twice the length and twice the width of the pillow. The width of the ruffle is twice the required finished depth plus 3cm/1¼in seam allowance.

you will need

- **pillow**
- **main fabric**
- **sewing kit**

tip for ruffled pillowcase
If you want to add embroidery, it is much easier to do this before the pillowcase is made up.

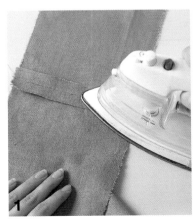
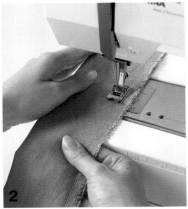

1 Cut sufficient strips of fabric to make the ruffle and join with flat seams. Join the strips into a complete circle. Press the seams flat.

2 Fold the ruffle lengthways with the seams to the inside and raw edges aligned and press. Fold the ruffle in four widthways and press to mark. Unfold, then work two rows of machine gathers along the raw edge, stopping and cutting the thread at each pressed mark. Knot one lot of thread ends in each quarter.

3 Mark the centre of each side on the front of the pillowcase and pin the joins in the gathers at these points, with raw edges aligned. Pull up the gathers evenly and tack (baste). Stitch the gathers 1cm/½in from the edge.

4 Make a 2cm/¾in double hem across each back piece on one side. Pin the main piece to the right side of the front and pin the flap on top, sandwiching the ruffle between the raw edges. Stitch around the edge. Trim and turn through.

pillowcase edgings

Add colour and pattern to plain bed linen by edging a pile of pillows with ribbon bands and bows. Bright ginghams work beautifully in a child's bedroom, but you could adapt the idea using cooler colours for a more sophisticated look.

you will need

- **plain white cotton pillowcases**
- **plain and gingham ribbons of various widths**
- **fusible bonding web**
- **baking parchment**
- **iron**
- **sewing kit**

tip for pillowcase edgings

When using fusible bonding web, always protect the ironing board and the iron with a layer of baking parchment. Place a sheet of parchment on the ironing board, put the fabric to be fused right side down on top, then place the fusible web mesh side down on top. Protect with a second sheet of baking parchment before applying the heat of the iron.

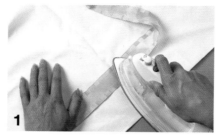

1 For the banded pillowcase, cut lengths of three different ribbons about 5cm/2in longer than the width of the pillowcase. Roughly cut three lengths of fusible bonding web slightly larger. Protect the ironing board with a sheet of baking parchment, then fuse the rough glue side of the web to one side of the ribbon, using the heat of an iron. Peel off the backing paper and trim the web from the ribbon. Position the ribbon on the pillowcase in the desired position and iron in place.

2 Turn in the raw edges and stitch the ribbons to the pillowcase at each end. Hand sew the long edges of the ribbon to the pillowcase.

3 For the pillowcase with ties, cut two 30cm/12in lengths from each of the five different narrow ribbons and pin one of each pair at regular intervals along the folded edge of the pillowcase opening. Stitch in place.

4 Using fusible bonding web, attach a length of wide ribbon to cover the ends of the ties. Hand or machine stitch around all the edges to secure.

5 Attach the matching ribbon lengths to the other side of the pillowcase opening, folding in the raw edges and stitching neatly to secure.

6 To decorate the pillowcase with ties, cut lengths of ribbon of differing widths and pin across the corners. Slip stitch to secure.

7 Fold the raw edges of the ribbons over on to the underside of the pillowcase. Cut a second length of each ribbon, fold in the ends to conceal the raw edges and slip stitch in place.

8 Finish the corner with a small ribbon bow, stitched through the knot to prevent it from coming undone.

heart-shaped cushion pad

Small, shaped cushions add interest rather than comfort to a group of scatter (throw) cushions. If you make the pad yourself the cushion can be any simple shape that you like. Stuff the pad with feathers, polyester stuffing or foam chips.

you will need
- paper and pencil for the template
- calico
- stuffing
- sewing kit

tip for heart-shaped cushion pad
Use a "featherproof" weight of calico to prevent feathers escaping from the cushion pad.

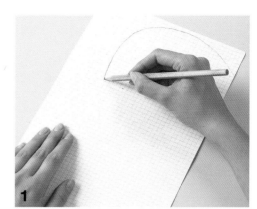

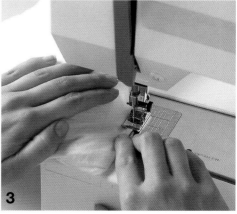

1 Draw the desired cushion shape on paper. Use this as a template to cut out two pieces of calico, including 1.5cm/⅝in seam allowance all round. Tack (baste) the two pieces together.

2 Stitch around the edge, leaving a gap along one of the straighter edges. If you are making a heart shape, snip into the "V" at the top and notch the curves. Turn through and stuff firmly with your chosen filling.

3 Pin the gap closed and stitch the edges together by machine, or slip-stitch the opening shut.

heart-shaped cushion cover

Making a shaped cushion cover is not difficult, especially if you have made the cushion pad yourself. It is actually very easy to make the pad, and that way you will be confident that the cover you make will be exactly the right shape and size.

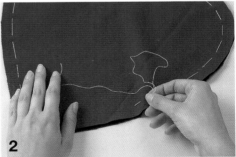

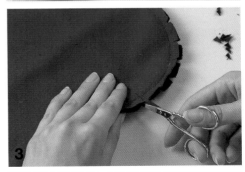

you will need

- paper and pencil to make the template
- velvet
- sewing kit

tip for heart-shaped cushion cover

If the cushion is quite large insert a zipper or make an envelope opening in the back across the widest part of the cover.

1 Draw round the cushion pad to make a paper template. Cut out two pieces to this size for the front and back covers, adding 1.5cm/⅝in seam allowance all round.

2 With right sides together, tack (baste) the two pieces together. Tacking is particularly important when using velvet as the fabric has a tendency to creep (move).

3 Stitch, leaving a large gap for inserting the cushion pad along one straighter side. Snip into the "V" at the top of the heart and along any inward-facing curves. Cut notches around the outward-facing curves, making the notches closer together on deeper curves. Trim across the point of the heart.

4 Turn the cushion cover through and insert the pad. Pin the gap closed and slip-stitch securely.

flat sheet

Flat sheets are versatile and can be used as a bottom or top sheet. When used as a top sheet, the top hem can be decorated with a piped edge, embroidery or a trimming. This will be visible when the sheet is folded over the bedcover or blanket.

above *Piping adds an unusual finish to the edge of a sheet.*

calculating the fabric

Measure the length, width and depth of the mattress. To work out the fabric size in each direction, add twice the mattress depth to the length and width, then add 50cm/20in to tuck in.

you will need

• **sheeting**

• **piping cord or ribbon (optional)**

• **sewing kit**

tip for flat sheet

You can make the two bottom corners fitted (see fitted sheet).

1 If the fabric is the width required leave the selvage down the sides; otherwise, stitch a 1.5cm/⅝in double hem down each side.

2 Along the bottom, make a 2.5cm/1in double hem and on the top edge press and stitch a 8cm/3in hem.

3 On the top edge stitch another row 5mm/¼in from the first to make a casing. Thread fine piping cord through the channel.

4 Alternatively finish the edge of the top hem with a pretty ribbon.

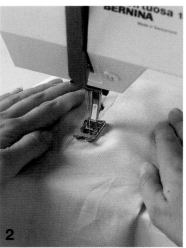

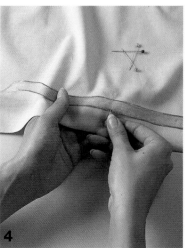

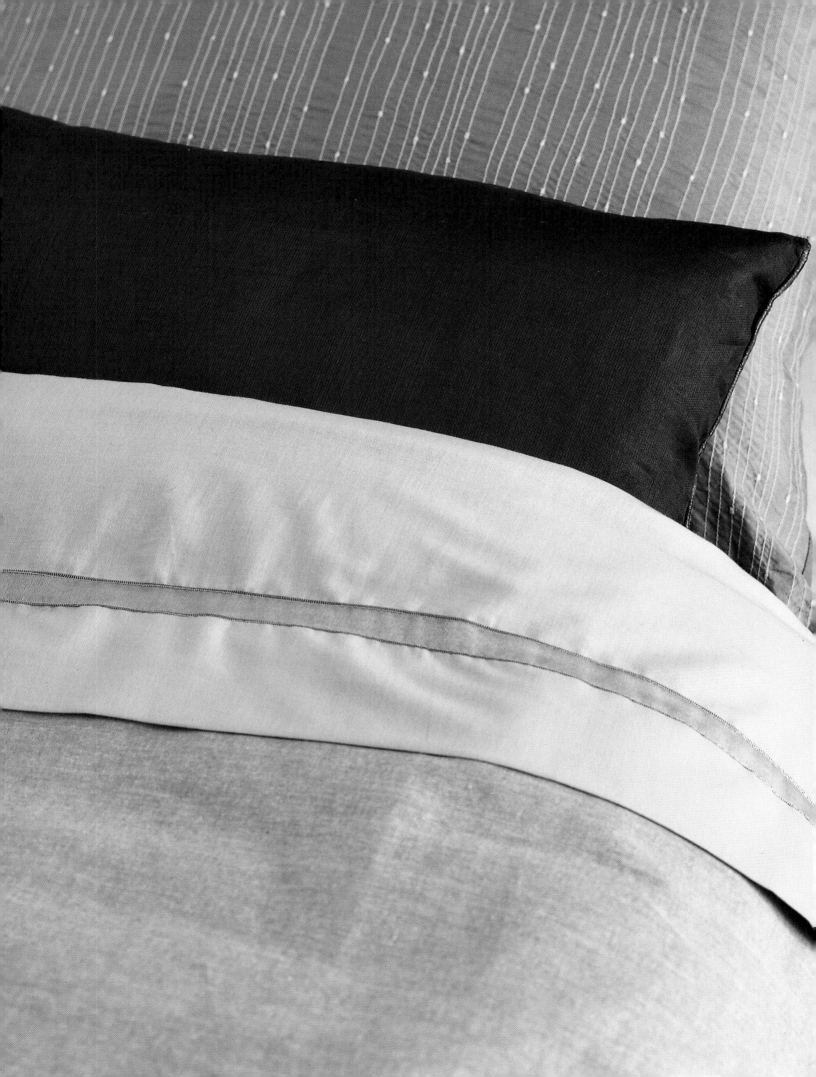

fitted sheet

A fitted sheet is made to fit snugly over the corners of the mattress and is ideal for beds with duvet covers. Make sure that you pre-shrink your fabric by washing it a couple of times at normal temperature first so that the sheet will not distort the mattress.

calculating the fabric

Measure the length, width and depth of the mattress. To work out the fabric size, add twice the mattress depth to the length and width, and then add another 36cm/14in to gather under the mattress.

you will need

- **sheeting**
- **tailor's chalk**
- **5mm /¼in elastic**
- **sewing kit**

tip for fitted sheet
Buy good quality elastic so that it lasts as long as the sheet.

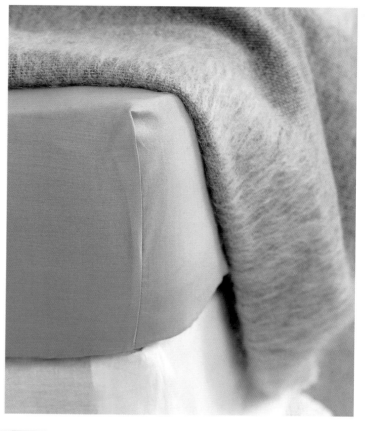

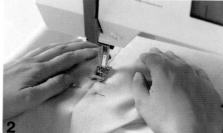

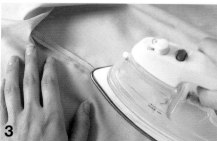

1 Cut the fabric the required size for the mattress and measure 36cm/14in along each side from the corners. Mark with tailor's chalk.

2 Fold the corners together to make a diagonal fold and match the marks. Fold the point to make a crease level with the marks. Pin and stitch along the crease on each corner. Tack (baste) first if you prefer and check the fit.

3 Trim the corner off leaving a 5mm/¼in seam allowance. Press the seam open and turn the fabric through. Press the seam flat and stitch 9mm/⅜in from the fold to complete the French seam.

4 Turn under and press a 1.5cm/⅝in double hem around the bottom of the sheet. This will form a channel to thread elastic through. Measure and mark 33cm/13in to each side of the corners. Stitch the hem leaving a small gap at each mark for threading the elastic.

5 Cut four lengths of 5mm/¼in elastic each 23cm/9in. Pin one end to the hem. Using a bodkin or safety pin, thread the elastic into the channel.

6 Pin the other end in place. Stitch across the hem securing the ends of the elastic in the stitching. Tuck the ends of the elastic just inside the opening and stitch the gap shut.

gathered valance (dust ruffle)

A bed valance (dust ruffle) can be used to hide storage boxes or disguise an unattractive bed base. A valance fits over the bed base under the mattress, and the flat, pleated or gathered skirt hangs down from this usually to the floor. A gathered valance gives a very soft, casual look to a bed. The base can be made from a cheaper fabric or old sheet as it is hidden under the mattress.

calculating the fabric

Measure the length and width of the mattress. To make the flat base, add 3cm/1¼in to the width and 3.5cm/1⅜in to the length. For the depth of the skirt, measure from the bottom edge of the mattress to the floor and add 5.5cm/2¼in. The skirt fits down the sides and across the base only, so to calculate its length add twice the width of the mattress to four times its length.

you will need

- **dinner plate**
- **sheeting or lightweight fabric**
- **tailor's chalk**
- **sewing kit**

tip for gathered valance (dust ruffle)
A gathered edge looks very pretty with a ribbon trim.

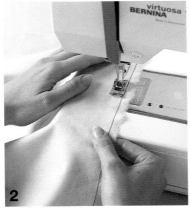

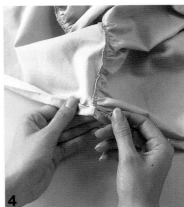

1 Cut fabric to fit the base including seam allowances. Use a dinner plate to round off the two corners that will sit at the bottom of the bed. Mark around the plate with tailor's chalk and cut neatly along the line.

2 For the skirt, cut and join sufficient lengths of fabric for the bottom and along each side. Join the sections of the skirt with French seams (see basic techniques) and mark into 1m/1yd sections along the top edge of the skirt. Stitch two rows of gathering stitches 1cm/½in apart, near the top raw edge, stopping, cutting the thread and restarting at each mark.

3 Mark every 50cm/20in down the sides and along the bottom edge of the base. Pin the skirt in place matching the marks. Pull the gathers up evenly and stitch 1.5cm/⅝in from the edge. Pull out the gathering threads and zigzag-stitch close to the stitching. Trim the seam allowance close to the zigzag.

4 Press the gathers towards the bed base. Pin and stitch a double 1cm/½in hem along the top of the base and down the ends of the skirt. Press and stitch a 2cm/¾in hem around the bottom of the skirt. The skirt can be decorated with a ribbon stitched on top of the stitched hem.

corner pleat valance (dust ruffle)

A corner pleat valance (dust ruffle) is more formal than a gathered valance and looks particularly good made up in linen or a brocade fabric.

calculating the fabric

Measure the length and width of the mattress. To make the flat base add 3cm/1¼in to the width and 3.5cm/1½in to the length. For the depth of the skirt, measure from the bottom edge of the mattress to the floor and add 5.5cm/2¼in. For the length of the skirt add twice the length to the width and then add 68cm/27in for the pleats and seam allowances.

you will need

- sheeting
- sewing kit

tip for corner pleat valance (dust ruffle)

For a less formal finish, attach a ribbon or tie to each side of the pleat and tie in a pretty bow.

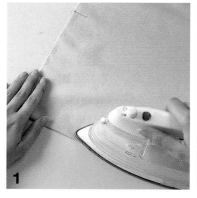

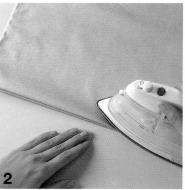

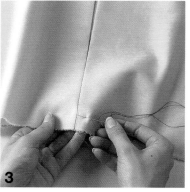

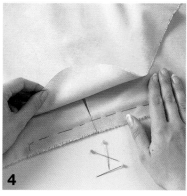

1 Measure the length of the bed plus 2cm/¾in along the skirt and mark with a pin. Insert another pin 32cm/12½in further along. Fold the fabric matching the pins and stitch a 2.5cm/1in seam. Press the fold.

2 Fold the top piece back on itself at the stitched point. Do the same at the other side and press the pleat. Measure along the width of the bed and do the same for the other corner.

3 Measure along the width of the bed and make a similar pleat for the other corner. Open out the pleats at the back. Pin the centre of the pleat behind the stitched seam. Press flat. Tack along the top edge to secure the pleat.

4 Curve the corners of the base panel, (a dinner plate is the ideal shape) and mark the centre of the curve. Match each mark to the centre of each pleat and pin all the way round. Stitch and finish as for the gathered valance.

box pleat valance (dust ruffle)

The box pleat valance (dust ruffle) is the most formal of the valances and looks particularly stylish in a crisp cotton or linen. Box pleats are essentially two knife pleats facing each other. The box pleats do not have to meet fold to fold, but can be narrow and spaced to give a lighter, jauntier appearance.

calculating the fabric

Measure the length and width of the mattress. To make the flat base add 3cm/1¼in to the width and 3.5cm/1½in to the length. For the depth of the skirt, measure from the bottom of the mattress to the floor and add 5.5cm/2¼in. For the length of the skirt add twice the length to the width and multiply by three then add 6cm/2½in.

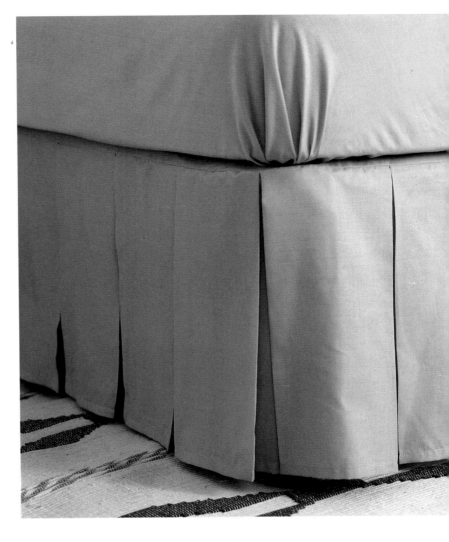

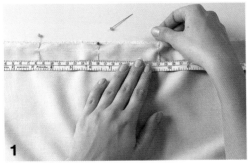

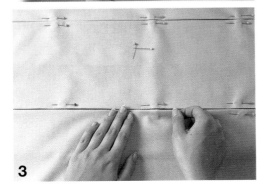

you will need
- sheeting
- sewing kit

calculating the pleats

Draw a diagram of the bed and work out how many and what size of pleat will fit across the base of the bed so that a pleat lies on each corner. The front of the pleat from fold to fold is the pleat width. Half that measurement is the pleat depth on the back.

1 Cut sufficient strips of fabric for the skirt and tack the seams. At one end, mark 3cm/1¼in for the side hem. Begin to mark the pleats beginning with a full pleat width and then two half widths. Continue along the full length of the skirt, marking the hem allowance at the other end. Any joins should be down the centre of two half widths. Adjust the length of the panels accordingly. Join the seams with French seams (see basic techniques).

2 Turn up a double 2cm/¾in hem and stitch. Cut the fabric to fit the mattress base and round off the corners as for the corner pleat valance.

3 Fold the pleats carefully so that the straight grain of the fabric runs down the edge. Press with a steam iron and then pin and tack (baste) each down its length. Complete as for the corner pleat valance.

duvet cover

One of the problems when making a duvet cover is finding fabric, other than standard sheeting, that is wide enough to make the front in one panel. Fabric can be joined with flat seams equally spaced down each side of a larger centre panel or with a single offset seam trimmed with piping.

you will need

- **main fabric**
- **piping cord**
- **fasteners such as buttons or popper (snap) tape**
- **sewing kit**

tip for duvet cover

Wash fabric before cutting out in case it shrinks.

1 Cut two panels for the front of the duvet cover so that the seam lies about one-third of the way across. Cover a length of piping cord to fit the length of the duvet cover and tack (baste) down the inside seam on one of the panels.

2 Pin the other panel on top and stitch close to the piping using a zipper foot. Press the seam allowance to one side. Join widths if required to make the back panel.

3 Turn and press a double 2.5cm/1in hem along the bottom edge of the back and front panels of the duvet.

4 To fasten the duvet with ties, cut four ties each 8 x 46cm/3 x 18in. Fold the strips in half lengthways and stitch a seam down the side and along the bottom. Turn the ties through and press. On the front and back bottom edges of the duvet, mark 30cm/12in from each side edge. Space two ties equally between the markers on the duvet front and back. Tuck the short raw edge of the ties into the hem and fold back over the seam. Pin in place.

5 Stitch the hem and the tie at the same time, stitching close to both folds.

6 With wrong sides together, pin the back and front of the duvet together. Stitch together around two long sides and the top using a 5mm/¼in seam. Press the seam open and turn through. Complete the French seam with a 9mm/⅜in seam allowance. Stitch 30cm/16in in from each side across the bottom of the duvet.

7 Alternatively, cut the popper (snap) tape 50cm/20in narrower than the width of the duvet. Centre the popper tape on the hem of one panel. Fit the other half on top, pin to the second hem and pull the tape apart. Stitch the popper tape and the hems at the same time. Stitch across the hems 25cm/10in from the edge of the duvet.

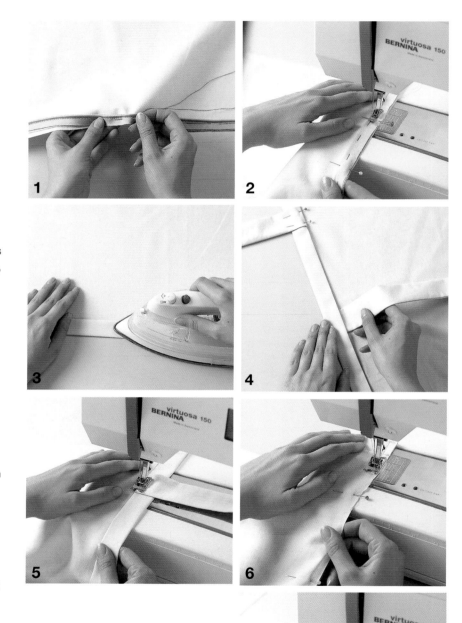

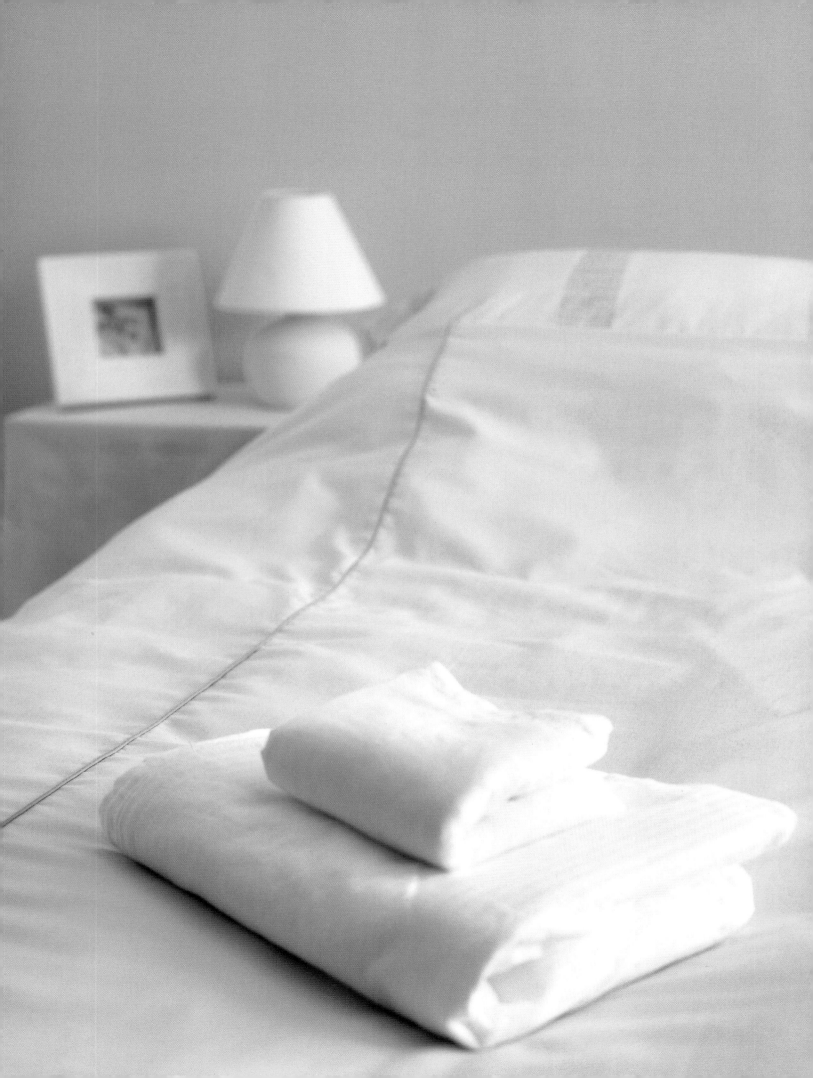

front envelope opening duvet cover

An envelope opening allows you to use a more unusual fabric for the front of the duvet cover because the textured surface doesn't lie next to your skin. The more suitable sheeting fabric can be used for the back and flap. The flap can be fastened with poppers (snaps) or pretty buttons and ribbon loops.

above *Use pretty buttons to finish.*

calculating the fabric

All panels are the width of the duvet plus 3cm/1¼in seam allowance. Cut the front panel the same length as the duvet plus 7cm/2¾in hem and seam allowance. Decide on the depth of the envelope flap and add this measurement to the length of the duvet back, adding 7cm/2¾in hem and seam allowance.

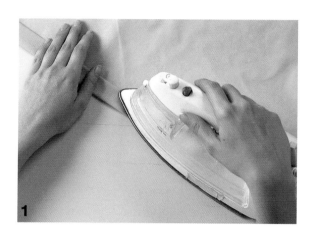

you will need

- **main fabric**
- **contrast fabric**
- **ribbon**
- **lightweight interfacing**
- **buttons**
- **sewing kit**

tip for front envelope opening duvet cover
Check that the fabric you use is suitable for a duvet cover.

1 Press a 2cm/¾in double hem across the bottom of the envelope flap. Press and stitch a 2cm/¾in double hem across the top of the main front panel.

2 For a single duvet, cut eight pieces of ribbon approximately 15cm/6in long for the button loops. Fold and press the ribbons to make a point as shown. Spacing the loops evenly across the duvet, tuck the raw ends under the hem and fold each back on itself and pin.

3 Stitch along the bottom edge to secure the ribbon loops of the hem. Add ribbon to the front of the hem. Stitch from the right side down each edge of the ribbon.

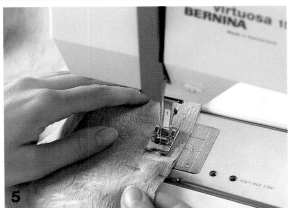

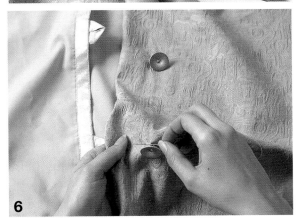

4 Lay the back panel with right side up and fold the flap over. Place the main panel on top with right side down.

5 Stitch the side seams and along the bottom, reverse-stitching at the top for extra strength. Zigzag-stitch the seams and turn the cover through.

6 Mark the position of the buttons on the front of the duvet. Press a square of interfacing behind each mark to strengthen the button fastening. Stitch the buttons in place.

fleece throw

A warm fleece throw is the simplest way to provide some extra warmth in the cold winter days. The edge of the fleece can be bound with a contrast fabric that complements the bed linen. Join the binding strips on the diagonal, preferably where the seam will be hidden in the mitre corners.

calculating the fabric

The length of the binding strips is twice the length and twice the width of the throw, plus seam allowances for joining strips and mitring corners.

you will need

- **fleece**
- **contrast lightweight fabric**
- **ribbon**
- **sewing kit**

tip for a fleece throw

Choose trimmings and fabrics that can be washed together.

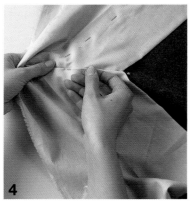
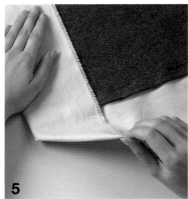
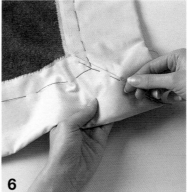

1 Cut the selvages off the fleece fabric. Cut the fleece to the exact size you require.

2 Decide on the width of the binding and cut four strips twice the finished width plus 3cm/1¼in seam allowance. Fold the strips in half widthways and press.

3 Open out the binding strips. Place the fleece right side up on top of one binding strip so that the edge of the fleece is level with the pressed crease. Pin and tack (baste) the fleece to the binding along the first side and close to the fold. Turn the fleece and binding over.

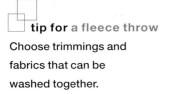
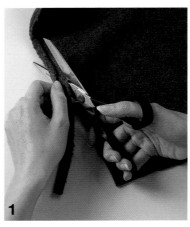

4 Turn under 1.5cm/⅝in along the front edge of the binding. Fold the binding over to make a neat mitre at the corner. Continue pinning and tacking the binding until all four sides and corners are complete.

5 Turn the throw over and fold the binding over to the right side. Fold the binding over at the corners to make a neat mitre.

6 Tack along the edge of the binding all around the throw. Slip-stitch the mitred corners in place on both sides and along the binding edge on the reverse.

7 Pin the ribbon to the front of the throw so that it overlaps the raw edge of the binding. Mitre the corners neatly. Stitch down each side of the ribbon. Stitch both sides in the same direction to prevent the ribbon twisting.

appliqué blanket

This brightly decorated blanket is certain to keep you warm. The appliqué motifs are all made of blanket fabric and stitched by hand with wool threads which give a bold, chunky feel to the design. If you are making the blanket for a child, leave out the beads and buttons and use extra embroidery stitches as embellishment instead.

you will need
- **soft pencil**
- **paper or thin cardboard**
- **paper scissors**
- **scraps of coloured blanket fabric**
- **vanishing fabric marker**
- **tapestry needle**
- **tapestry wool or knitting wool (yarn), in different colours**
- **assorted beads**
- **small coloured buttons**
- **blanket**
- **sewing kit**

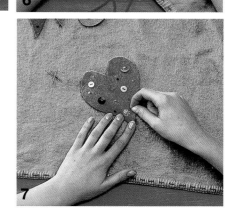

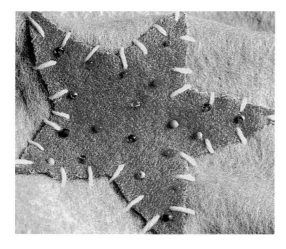

right *Beads add interest to the shapes, but you could use any small objects such as buttons, sequins and ribbons.*

1 Draw a heart and star on paper or thin cardboard to the required size. Draw around the templates on to the coloured blanket fabrics, using a fading fabric marker and cut out.

2 Embroider some of the hearts and stars with French knots, using wool in contrasting colours

3 Embroider the remaining hearts and stars with decorative cross stitches in contrasting colours.

4 Stitch assorted beads on to some of the appliqué shapes. Be careful to attach them securely.

5 Stitch buttons to the other shapes and embroider with more decorative stitches, using wool threads.

6 Work a line of decorative running stitch along each end of the blanket in contrasting wool.

7 Smooth out the blanket on a clean flat surface and arrange the heart and star shapes on it. Pin in place.

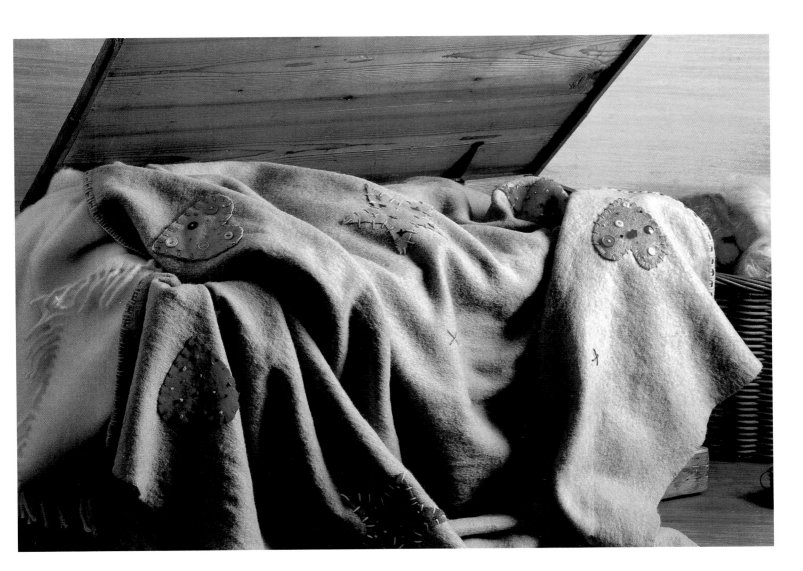

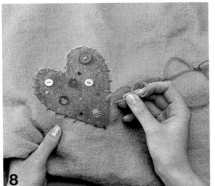

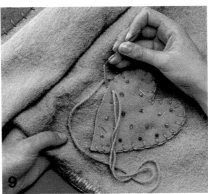

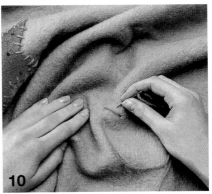

8 Stitch some of the shapes on to the blanket, using stab stitch (an individual running stitch that can be any length) and a contrasting wool.

9 Stitch the remaining shapes on to the blanket, using blanket stitch, or any other decorative stitch of your choice.

10 Fill in the background of the blanket with individual large cross stitches in brightly coloured threads.

quilted bedspread

This quick and easy patchwork quilt can be made in a weekend. The large panels of mixed blue-and-white fabric give the quilt a classic look and the layers are simply tied together at intervals. Achieving a random look to the quilt is not as easy as you might think. Lay out the cut squares and rectangles on the floor and rearrange until you achieve a colour and fabric balance.

calculating the fabric

Measure the bed and allow 30–50cm/12–20in for an overhang on the sides and end of the quilt. You will need at least five different fabrics for the quilt top. Work out how many square metres/yards will fit on the quilt and buy sufficient fabric allowing a little extra for seam allowances. The wadding (batting) has to be slightly larger than the finished quilt size and the backing fabric, 16cm/6¼in larger all round.

you will need

- selection of cotton fabrics in a similar weight for the patches
- fabric for the borders
- backing fabric
- 50g/2oz wadding (batting)
- quilting pins
- crochet cotton
- sewing kit

tip for quilted bedspread
If required, join widths of wadding with herringbone stitch.

1 To plan the panels for the quilt front, take 16cm/6¼in from the proposed width of the quilt and divide by three. Add 12mm/½in to this for the centre panel and add 9cm/3½in for the two outside panels. Cut squares and rectangles of different fabrics to these widths and sew together with 5mm/¼in seams.

2 Press the seams towards the darker fabric. Pin the three rows together and stitch with 5mm/¼in seams. Press the seams towards the darker side. If necessary, snip into the seam and press different sections in opposite directions. Press the quilt top.

3 Place the quilt backing on a clean, flat surface. On top centre the wadding (batting). Centre the quilt top on the wadding and smooth out. Check that the backing is 15cm/6in from the raw edge of the quilt top.

4 Beginning in the centre and working out in a ray pattern, tack (baste) the layers together with long stitches. Measure and mark the position of the ties so that they are regularly spaced over the quilt – about 15–20cm/6–8in apart. Using crochet cotton take a small stitch through all layers, leaving a 10cm/4in tail. Take a back stitch, then bring the needle out at the front. Tie the ends in a reef (square) knot.

5 Trim the wadding only to match the quilt top. Fold the raw edge of the backing in to meet the raw edge of the quilt top and press the edge.

6 Open out the hem. Trim across the diagonal line. Fold the corner at the pressed crease lines. Refold the binding into the original folds to make a double hem with a neat double mitred corner.

7 Slip-stitch the edge of the binding to the quilt top. For a more secure finish, the edge of the binding can be stitched through all layers with a decorative row of white running stitch. Slip-stitch along the mitred corners to complete the quilt.

bed drape

This lovely decoration gives a stunning look to a bed. Sheer fabric is gathered on to a hoop, which can be attached to the wall or suspended by cord from the ceiling. The ideal cane to use is kooboo cane, which is very pliable and can be bent into a circle.

above *Very flimsy, lightweight fabrics may need curtain weights to hold them in place.*

calculating the fabric

Measure from the proposed height of the hoop down to the floor and add 10cm/4in seam allowance. Allow 3–4 widths of fabric to give sufficient fullness, especially if the bed has a headboard.

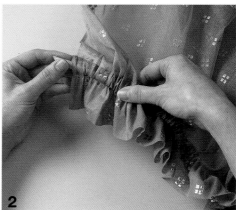

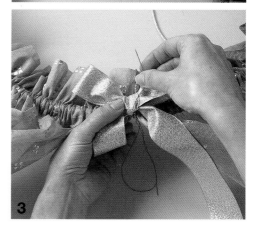

you will need

- sheer fabric
- pliable cane to make into a ring
- strong cord or neutral colour adhesive tape
- ribbon (optional)
- cord for hanging
- sewing kit

tip for bed drape

For a different effect decorate the hoop with extra twisted fabric.

1 Press under an 8cm/3in hem along the top edge of each fabric width and stitch. Stitch a second row to make a casing deep enough to fit the cane hoop. Cut the cane to the required length, shaping the ends at an acute angle. Thread the cane through the casing.

2 Bend the cane into a circle, overlapping the cut ends. Bind the ends securely together with strong cord or adhesive tape. Tie a length of cord at the gap between each width of fabric. (The cord should be long enough to reach the ceiling.)

3 Check the length of the drape then stitch a 5mm/¼in double hem along the bottom edge. If desired, attach a ribbon bow at the front. Tie the cords at the required height and suspend from the ceiling.

a flat canopy for a bed

A flat canopy is a more dramatic way to decorate a four-poster bed. The fabric softens the hard frame of the bed and creates a tent-like, intimate effect, as the "ceiling" is lowered. The canopy hangs down to the bottom of the mattress at the head of the bed, over the top of the bed frame and down a short distance at the foot of the bed. The amount the drape hangs at the foot depends on the depth of the bed frame. Tie the canopy with ribbons and insert curtain weights in the front two corners so that it hangs straight.

calculating the fabric

Drape a long piece of rope or chain weight over the ends of the bed posts or along the side of the bed to find out what length of fabric is required to drape from one end to the other. Add the short drop at the front and the distance from the bedpost to the mattress at the head of the bed. The canopy can be as wide as the bed or a narrower strip as shown here.

you will need

- **main fabric**
- **ribbon**
- **curtain weights**
- **sewing kit**

tip for a flat canopy for a bed
Use Velcro on the posts to prevent the canopy slipping.

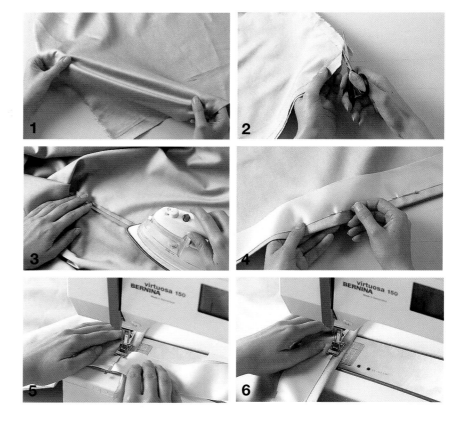

1 It is essential that the fabric is absolutely square before beginning to make a bed canopy, so that it hangs correctly once it is in place. Pull a thread to straighten one end and fold the fabric in half lengthways – if the corners don't match pull the fabric on the diagonal until it is straight. You may need to work all the way down the fabric. Press the straightened folded fabric with a steam iron.

2 Cut two pieces of fabric the required size including a 1.5cm/⅝in seam allowance on all sides. With right sides together, stitch around all sides leaving a large gap for turning along the edge that will go behind the bed. Trim across the corners.

3 Trim the seams to 5mm/¼in and press open as far as possible into each corner. Turn the canopy through and roll the edges until the seam is exactly on the edge and press again.

4 Pin the ribbon down each side of the canopy. Place pins exactly on the edge as pins will mark satin ribbon. Leave enough ribbon at the foot end of the canopy to stitch on the other side of the overhang. Pin the ribbon in place on the underside of the canopy.

5 To fasten the canopy to the bed head, cut two lengths of ribbon each 1m/1yd long and fold in half. Stitch in place at the corners at the head of the canopy, in each corner, for example. The other end of the canopy will hang loosely over a pole or the bed post. Drop a curtain weight in to each front corner, then slip-stitch the gap closed.

6 Stitch down both sides of the ribbon. Stitch each side in the same direction to prevent the ribbon twisting. Fold the excess ribbon up on the other side and stitch so that you machine stitch on top of the previous stitches.

adding lace to a bed canopy

If the canopy is lined, the lace can be inserted between the fabric and the lining. If the canopy is a single layer, the lace should be attached with a type of lapped seam to hide any raw edges.

you will need
- **main fabric**
- **lace**
- **ribbon**
- **sewing kit**

tip for adding lace to a bed canopy

Lace-edged fabric looks particularly effective hanging from a corona.

canopies

A simple canopy is a length of fabric that drapes comfortably over the head and foot of the bed. It can be draped over bed posts, or hung over a length of dowel suspended from the ceiling. Soft fabrics look good draping in pools at the foot of the bed, so be generous with your fabric quantities.

1 Pin the lace and the canopy fabric wrong sides together. Stitch, leaving a 5mm/¼ in seam.

2 Open the lace and fabric out and press the seam in towards the canopy fabric.

3 Pin a length of ribbon over the raw edges of the seam on the right side. Stitch down both sides of the ribbon, stitching each side in the same direction to prevent puckering.

a corona with fixed drapes

A corona looks extremely impressive, but in fact it is simply a curtain and a pelmet attached to a semi-circular pelmet board. Here a soft, lace-trimmed valance covers the top of the curtain, which hangs from hooks underneath the pelmet board. The curtain can simply drape down each side of the bed, or can continue across the back of the bed as well.

you will need

- pencil
- wooden board for the corona base 25 x 12.5 x 2.5cm/10 x 5 x 1in
- jigsaw
- sandpaper
- staples and staple gun
- adhesive Velcro
- hammer
- galvanized staples
- brackets
- fabric
- Velcro heading tape
- lace
- curtain hooks
- sewing kit

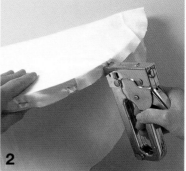

1 Draw a semi-circular pattern the required width of the corona on to a piece of wooden board, with the depth from the straight edge about 25cm/10in. Cut out with a jigsaw and sand the edges.

2 Using a staple gun, cover the board with fabric, stapling into the curved edge.

3 Adhere the hook side of Velcro tape around the curved edge, ensuring it is firmly stuck. Secure with staples.

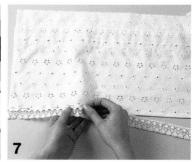

4 Hammer galvanized staples all the way around the underside of the board, about 2.5cm/1in from the edge. Leave gaps and attach two brackets to the straight edge for fixing the corona to the wall.

5 Cut the valance (dust ruffle) fabric three to four times longer than the curved edge of the board, adding 7cm/2¾in seam allowance to the depth. Press under 6cm/2⅛in to the wrong side along the top edge. Stitch a 5mm/¼in double hem along each short side edge. Press any seams open.

6 Pin a 5cm/2in-wide Velcro heading tape along the top of the valance, 5cm/2in from the pressed edge. Trim the tape at the end of the valance and fold under the raw end. Tuck the ends of the tape cords underneath at one side and leave loose at the other. Stitch round the edge of the tape.

7 Press under a 5mm/¼in hem along the bottom edge. Pin lace to the right side of the edge and stitch in place. Draw up the tape cords to fit the corona board and attach the valance to the Velcro.

to make the curtain

Measure around the whole corona board and make a curtain two to three times wider. Stitch a simple 2.5cm/1in-wide heading tape along the top edge. Insert one curtain hook for each galvanized staple and gather the curtain to fit. Beginning in the middle of the curved edge of the board, hang the curtain on to the corona.

tied headboard cover

A tied cover is the simplest type of cover for headboards. It is essentially a flat piece of fabric that is tied at the sides with ribbon bows. This style of cover is only suitable for square or rectangular shaped headboards.

above *Sheer ribbon adds a feminine touch.*

calculating the fabric

Measure the width of the headboard and add 3cm/1⅛in seam allowance. Measure from the base of the headboard over the top and down the other side.

you will need

- **slim, squared-up headboard**
- **main fabric**
- **contrast lining**
- **plate**
- **tailor's chalk**
- **bias binding**
- **ribbon**
- **sewing kit**

tip for tied headboard cover
Join the binding lengths together with a diagonal seam.

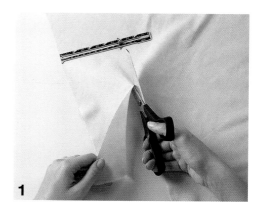

1 Cut one piece of main fabric and one in a contrast lining. Put a plate at each corner and draw around the curve with tailor's chalk, from raw edge to raw edge. Place the lining and fabric wrong sides together and tack (baste) around the edge. Cut and join sufficient strips of bias binding, 9cm/3½in wide, to fit around the cover.

2 With wrong sides together, fold the bias strip in half lengthways and press. With raw edges aligned pin and tack the binding to the right side of the cover. Stitch 1.5cm/⅝in from the edge.

3 Turn the binding to the wrong side and pin in place, easing binding round the corners neatly.

4 To make the ties, cut 12 lengths of ribbon, each 40cm/16in. Fold the cover in half. At each side measure and mark about 10cm/4in from the top and bottom of the cover and in the middle. Tuck a piece of ribbon inside the binding at each mark and pin. Slip-stitch the binding to the lining, securing the ribbon in the stitching.

shaped headboard cover

This type of cover is suitable for a fairly slim headboard as it is made without a gusset. The thin wadding (batting) covers any buttons or padding on the original headboard.

you will need

- 50g/2oz wadding (batting)
- felt-tipped pen
- main fabric
- contrast fabric
- piping cord
- ribbon
- sewing kit

tip for shaped headboard cover

Use a flanged cord instead of piping for a different effect.

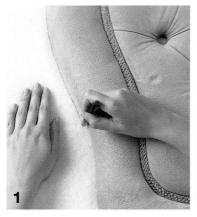

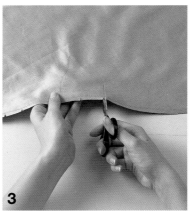

1 Place a large piece of 50g/2oz wadding (batting) on a flat surface. Place the headboard on top. Draw around the edge with a felt-tipped pen, adding 0.5–1cm/¼–⅜in on all sides. Cut out, adding a 1.5cm/⅝in seam allowance around the edge. Cut two pieces each of wadding, main fabric and lining the same size.

2 Cover sufficient piping cord to fit around the curved edges of the headboard. Pin each piece of wadding to the wrong side of a piece of main fabric. Tack (baste) and stitch the piping round the curved edge. Stitch the second side on top.

3 Stitch the lining sections together and trim the seams. Snip the inward facing curves and notch the outward curves of the lining and headboard cover.

4 Slip the lining over the wadding side of the headboard cover. Cut four lengths of ribbon each 25cm/10in, and pin between the layers along the bottom edge, two on each side. Match the side seams. Pin then stitch around the bottom edge, leaving a large gap for turning. Turn through, tuck the lining inside and slip-stitch the gap closed. Slip the cover over the headboard and tie the ribbons.

box-style headboard cover

This style of cover has a gusset to fit a deep headboard with a square edge. The piping adds an interesting detail and defines the shape of the cover. If using a patterned fabric, the gusset will have a seam in the centre at the top so that the pattern matches down the sides.

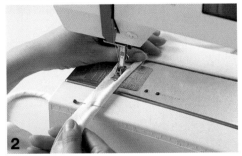

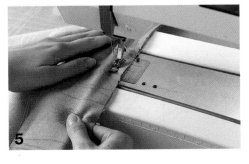

you will need

- pencil
- calico for template
- main fabric
- piping cord
- contrast fabric for piping
- fusible bonding web (optional)
- sewing kit

1 Make a template from calico by drawing around the headboard. Cut the template out adding a 1.5cm/⅝in seam allowance around the edge. Fold the template in half and position the fold down the centre of any pattern. Open out and pin in position.

2 Cover sufficient piping to fit around the edge at the front and back of the headboard cover.

3 With raw edges aligned, pin and tack (baste) the piping around the edge of the cover. Snip the piping at the corners so that it fits smoothly.

4 Cut the gusset the width of the sides, adding 3cm/1¼in seam allowance. On patterned fabric, cut the gusset in two pieces. Pin in position, matching the pattern from the bottom edge up to the centre on each side. Sew the centre seam.

5 Stitch the gusset as close as possible to the piping on the headboard front using a zipper foot attachment. Pin the back cover to the other side of the gusset, matching the corners, and stitch in place. Turn up the bottom hem and slip-hem or stick with fusible bonding web. Add ties at the bottom if required.

cot (crib) quilt

A baby needs to be warm but not too hot – duvets are not suitable and many quilts are bulky.
This quilt is light and easy to wash and it keeps its shape because of the machine-quilting stitches.

calculating the fabric

Measure the inside of the cot, allowing 50cm/20in at the top for
the baby's head. Add 8cm/3in allowance to each side.

you will need

- lightweight cotton fabric
- 50g/2oz wadding (batting)
- contrast fabric for the frill
- backing fabric
- sewing kit

tip for cot (crib) quilt
You could use ribbon or lace
to make the frill.

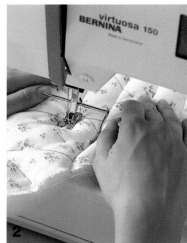

1 Place the fabric right side up on top of the wadding (batting) and pin in place. Tack
(baste) the layers parallel to the sides as well as diagonally.

2 Fit a quilting foot and a quilting guide to the sewing machine. Set the guide to
stitch rows 3–4cm/1½–1¾in apart. Begin in one corner and stitch diagonally
across the quilt.

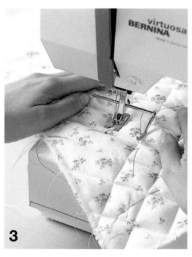

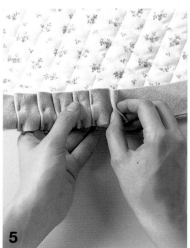

3 Turn the quilt and stitch back in the other direction to make a diamond pattern.
Use your hands to guide the fabric so that no tucks form in the quilt top as you
are stitching.

4 Decide on the depth of the pleated frill. Cut bias strips, twice the desired
finished width, adding 3cm/1½in seam allowance. To calculate the length,
measure the diameter of the quilt. You will need 2–3 times the measurement
depending on how frilled you want the edge to be.

5 Pin the frill along the sides and bottom edge of the quilt. Make the pleats by
eye, folding and pinning them in place. Adjust any that are not quite straight.
Stitch the frill in place.

6 Place the lining on top and pin and stitch in place around the edge leaving
a gap along the bottom edge. Trim across the corners and turn the quilt
through. Press the top edge with a cool iron and top stitch the top edge.
Slip-stitch the gap.

lined baby basket

There is so much paraphernalia for babies that you can never have enough storage. Make a pretty quilted liner for a layette basket to match the cot (crib) quilt and use it to store baby clothes or nappy changing materials.

calculating the fabric

Measure the inside bottom of the basket, adding 1.5cm/⅝in seam allowance to each edge. Measure the height of the basket and around the outside top edge for the side panels.

you will need

- **fabric**
- **50g/2oz wadding (batting)**
- **contrast fabric for frill and ties**
- **bodkin or rouleau turner**
- **sewing kit**

tip for lined baby basket
Use ribbon or lace for the frills and ties for a more delicate effect.

1 Cut a piece of fabric and wadding (batting) larger than the inside measurements of the sides of the basket you want to line. Machine quilt in a diamond pattern (see cot quilt). Tuck the panel into the basket inside out and pin a seam down one corner. Pin darts down the other corners. Stitch the darts.

2 Pin and stitch the pleated frill along the top edge of the right side of the fabric, with raw edges aligned (see cot quilt). With right sides together, stitch lining the same size as the quilting along the frill edge. Open the quilting and lining out and fold crossways with the frill facing the lining. Stitch a seam on the quilted side only. Fold the lining to the outside and slip-stitch the seam. Stitch the frill ends together.

3 Fold a 1m/1yd strip of 3cm/1¼in wide fabric in half and stitch 5mm/¼in from the folded edge. Turn the tube through using a bodkin or rouleau turner. Cut the rouleau in half. Tie knots in the end and stitch the middle of each piece to the end of the basket liner.

4 Tie the rouleaux through the basket handles in a pretty bow. To complete the basket, cut a piece of wadding to cover the base of the basket and cover with fabric. Tuck into the base of the basket.

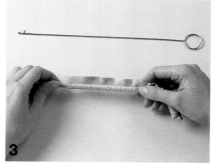

covering a Moses basket

A Moses basket is an ideal temporary bed for a newborn baby. The sides of the basket protect the baby from draughts while allowing air to circulate through the weave.

you will need

- **Moses basket**
- **150g/6oz wadding (batting)**
- **lightweight cotton fabric**
- **ribbon for the bows**
- **lace for edging**
- **5mm/¼in elastic**
- **sewing kit**

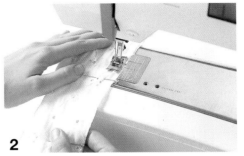

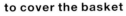

to cover the basket

1. Cut a piece of 150g/5oz wadding (batting) the depth of the basket, adding 10cm/4in to turn over the top edge and long enough to fit around the inside of the basket, adding 5–10cm/2–4in for ease. Cut into the wadding at each side of the handles and cut across between the slits, level with the top of the basket.

2. Measure right around the top of the basket. Cut a strip of fabric one and a half times the length plus 3cm/1¼in seam allowance and 66cm/26in deep. The depth measurement includes a generous tuck-in allowance. Fold the fabric in half crossways. To shape the cover, mark 10cm/4in along the bottom edge from the fold and cut diagonally to the top edge. Stitch a French seam (see basic techniques). Shape and stitch the seam at the other end of the cover in the same way.

3. To make the outside frill, turn up a 10cm/4in hem along the lower edge of the fabric and press. Stitch the hem and then stitch again 1cm/½in from the first line of stitching to make a casing for the elastic, leaving a gap at the seam to thread the elastic through later. Turn under and stitch a 1cm/½in double hem along the bottom edge.

4. For the holes for the handles, measure the width of the handles and add 2.5cm/1in for ease (a).

5. Measure the height of the basket at its lowest (b) and highest (c) point. Measure the basket from the top centre round the side to the handle. Multiply this measurement by one and a half to find the distance (d) to mark the handle from the top French seam.

▷

6 Arrange the cover flat with a French seam at each end and the hem at the top. Insert a pin the distance (d) from the right seam and the measurement (b) down from the hem.

7 Mark the other end of the handle hole, measurement (a) across to the left, and distance (c) down from the hem edge. To make the handle holes, cut a sloping oval between

the marks about 5cm/2in wide through both layers. Carefully turn under the raw edges around each to make a narrow rolled hem and slip-stitch.

8 Cut two 30cm/12in lengths of ribbon and hand stitch each to the middle of each side of the handle hole. Tie the ribbons in a bow.

9 Cut a piece of elastic, 10cm/4in shorter than the circumference of the basket and thread through the casing by pinning with a safety pin one end of the elastic to one end of the casing, and threading the other end of the elastic through a bodkin. Tie the ends securely and tuck inside the casing. Slip-stitch the gap.

10 Pin lace around the edge of the frill and machine stitch in place, turning in the raw edges at each short end. Insert the wadding (batting) into the basket. Fit the cover over the handles with the frill on the outside and arrange the gathers evenly.

11 To make a matching quilt, remove the mattress and draw around it. Add 1.5cm/⅝in all round for seams and cut out. Lay the fabric right sides together with the wadding on top and pin. Stitch around the edge, leaving a gap on one side for turning through.

12 Trim the wadding neatly and notch the curves. Turn the quilt through, pushing out the corners and slip-stitch the gap. Tie a ribbon bow and stitch it to the top of the quilt. Tie three ribbon bows and stitch one to the top of the quilt and one at each end of the Moses basket.

table linen

Table linen can be practical or luxurious and made in either plain fabric or something quite exquisite, depending on how you intend it to be used. Choose easy-care cotton fabrics for everyday use, but look for more luxurious fabrics and trimmings for special occasions. There are so many kinds of table linen that can be used to make your table look really special, including fine cottons and linens or rich velvets for a Christmas table setting. Use simple quilted mats for family meals, formal white linen to cover a long table for a buffet, or make a set of specially decorated napkins for a dinner party. Simple appliqué makes a table runner look unique and makes ordinary cotton look special.

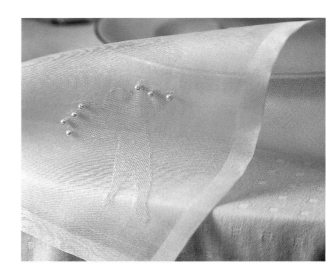

above left Add a subtle decorative touch using appliqué and pearl beads on crisp, sheer fabrics to make a stunning table runner or set of place mats.

centre above Blue-and-white check seersucker fabric makes a delightful and easy-care tablecloth for the breakfast table.

above right Pure raw and bleached linen are timeless fabrics that look stunning on any table. Drawn thread work is the traditional technique for hems and decoration.

centre left Choose co-ordinating velvet ribbons to tie around exotic brocade napkins instead of napkin rings for a special dinner party.

below left Napkins do not have to be made in plain fabrics. Pre-pleated and other textured fabrics add contrast to smooth china plates.

right Exotic fabrics and trimmings transform a plain table for a special occasion.

Whether for everyday use or a special occasion, table linen is primarily designed to protect the table from spillages, knocks and hot dishes. This doesn't mean necessarily that the fabrics need to be particularly heavyweight, as the table itself can be protected with a heat-resistant material or pad hidden under a pretty tablecloth. Nevertheless, table linen must be practical and has to be suitable for cleaning. The more often it is used, the easier it should be to wash and press. Indeed easy-care items that don't need to be ironed are the most suitable for everyday use.

There are lots of different ways that you can cover a table. As well as a tablecloth, there is the table runner, which is a strip of fabric that lies along the centre of the table. A table runner can act as a continuous tablemat down the centre of the table at a dinner party or be left to decorate the table during the day.

Tablemats are, at their simplest, a rectangle of fabric large enough to hold a dinner plate but can also be padded or quilted to protect the table from heat. It depends on the material your table is made from. Thin tablemats can always be used over a tablecloth with a heat-resistant cover underneath, but simple quilted tablemats that can be washed and quickly tumbled dry are more suitable for family meals.

Napkins are simply squares of fabric. Make them in a generous size, as they are much more practical. Although normally only used for special occasions nowadays, you might find that a set of easy-care napkins for family meals would reduce your clothes washing.

rectangular tablecloth

The deep border adds weight around the edge of this linen tablecloth, which helps to keep it flat and prevents it from slipping off the table. Make it in easy-care fabric for everyday dining, or in linen for special occasions, or as a day cover for the table top.

calculating the fabric

Measure the length and width of the table, then subtract 11cm/4½in from each measurement to allow for the border. Add twice the desired overhang to each measurement.

you will need

- fabric
- contrast fabric
- sewing kit

tip for rectangular tablecloth

Make sure the border and main fabrics are compatible for laundering.

1 Cut out the main fabric. For the border, cut four strips of contrast fabric 28cm/11in wide and 22cm/9in longer than the main fabric. Fold in half lengthways and press. Open out the folds.

2 With right sides together and raw edges aligned, centre the border strips along the edges of the main fabric. Stitch from the main fabric side, beginning and finishing 1.5 cm/⅝ in from the corner.

3 At each corner, fold one border on top of the other then fold the border diagonally to mark the stitching line. Stitch from the corner of the main fabric out to the foldline in the centre of the border.

4 Trim the seam and press. Fold the border fabric to the wrong side and mitre the corner, trimming the excess fabric at each side of the diagonal seam. Stitch or slip-stitch the reverse side hem. Slip-stitch the mitred corner to complete the tablecloth.

circular tablecloth

Circular tablecloths can be made any size, to fit your table. A cloth for a dining table should hang down to the level of your knees when sitting at the table, but bedside or living room tablecloths often reach the floor. If the fabric isn't wide enough join an equal amount to each side, leaving the main width of fabric in the centre, to make the seams less obvious.

calculating the fabric

Measure the diameter of the table and add twice the proposed overhang to this measurement plus 5cm/2in seam allowance. This is the tablecloth diameter. Cut a square of fabric 5cm/2in larger than this to allow plenty of room for marking the circle.

you will need

- fabric
- string
- pencil
- contrast fabric
- sewing kit

tip for circular tablecloth
Stitch around just inside the marked line before cutting to prevent the edge stretching.

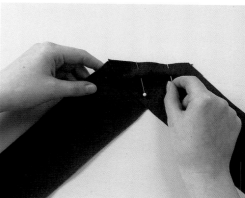

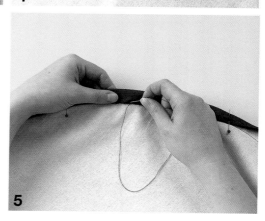

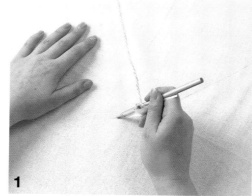

1 Fold the main fabric in four to make a quarter-size square and press lightly, matching the folds. Tie a length of string to a pencil and secure the end to the corner of the fabric so that the string length is half the tablecloth diameter. Keeping the string taut, draw a line in a quarter circle on the folded fabric. Cut along the line.

2 To work out the circumference of the tablecloth, multiply the diameter of the cloth by 3.14. Using contrast fabric, cut and join sufficient bias strips, 8cm/3in wide, to make a binding long enough to go around the tablecloth edge.

3 Press the binding strip in half lengthways with wrong sides together, then press the raw edges into the crease. Fold again and press the strip into a gentle curve.

4 Open out one edge of the binding and pin it around the edge of the tablecloth, with raw edges aligned and right sides together. Join the ends of the binding with a diagonal seam. Stitch the binding along the first crease. Press.

5 Turn the binding to the wrong side of the tablecloth and pin. Hem the cloth, stitching into the previous stitches. Press on the wrong side with a steam iron.

appliqué napkins

Appliqué does not have to be intricate, complex or time-consuming. Even the simplest design, trimming the ends of a napkin, can give it a more finished look. Use ready-made napkins, or make them yourself from 30cm/12in squares of fabric.

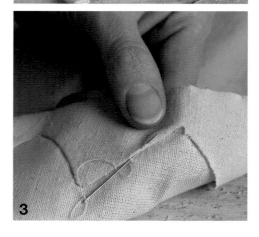

you will need

- **lime-coloured napkin**
- **paper scissors**
- **paper**
- **iron**
- **ironing board**
- **6 lemon-coloured napkins**
- **sewing kit**

1 Cut a 5cm/2in wide strip off one side of the lime napkin and fold it in half crossways, in half again and in half a third time. Cut a piece of paper to this width, and then fold it in half and snip off one corner. Open out the paper and use it as a template to cut the corners of the folded lime strip. Open out the zigzag edging.

2 Fold over a 1cm/¼in hem along the full length of the lime strip and along the short ends. Using a hot iron, press the hem into position. Neatly slip-stitch the straight edge of the lime strip to the edge of the lemon napkin.

3 Slip-stitch the zigzag edge of the strip to the napkin, turning in the edges as you go. You will only need to turn in these edges very slightly – just enough to neaten them – or you may find it difficult to create the "points" at the inner and outer corners of the zigzag.

chenille napkin tassels

Chenille tassels add a glamorous finishing touch to napkins and tablecloths. They are easy to make, and there is a wide choice of colours in chenille knitting yarns.

you will need

- **ball of chenille knitting yarn**
- **scissors**
- **darning needle**
- **napkins**

1 Make a 15cm/6in skein of chenille to half the desired thickness of the finished tassel. Cut a separate short length of chenille.

2 Fold the skein over the short length of chenille (this will be used to sew the tassel to the napkin). Cut another length of chenille.

3 Wind this second piece of chenille around the top of the skein and secure the end. Trim the bottom of the tassel. Use the "hanging" yarn to sew the tassel to the corner of the napkin.

bound-edge napkins

A contrast binding is a classic way to finish the edge of a napkin. Use a fairly thin fabric for the binding so that the corners are not too bulky and can be easily stitched in place by sewing machine. This is a very simple project to tackle.

calculating the fabric

Allow a 38cm/15in square of fabric for each napkin. You will need a 16 x 40cm/6 x 16in piece of fabric for the binding.

you will need

• **fabric**
• **contrast fabric**
• **sewing kit**

tip for bound-edge napkins

Trim the seam allowance on the binding at the corners to reduce bulk.

 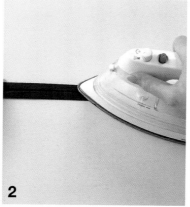 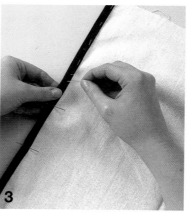 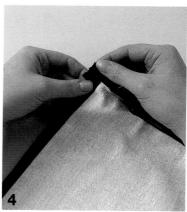

1 To cut the main fabric, snip into the selvage and pull a thread, then cut along the line. Measure 38cm/15in intervals along the selvage and repeat the process. Measure along the cut edge and pull a thread to complete the squares.

2 For each napkin, cut four binding strips each 4 x 40cm/1½ x 16in from contrast fabric. With wrong sides together, press the strips in half lengthways, then fold the raw edges into the centre and press again.

3 Tuck a strip of binding down two opposite sides of the napkin and tack (baste) in place, checking that you catch the binding on the wrong side in the stitching. Stitch close to the inside folded edge.

4 Trim the binding flush with the edge of the napkin. Pin the other two pieces of binding in place. Turn the short ends in at the corners and tack. Stitch as before, reverse-stitching at each end.

quilted placemats

Placemats are very practical for everyday eating as they can be washed quickly ready for the next meal. Any washable fabric is suitable but pre-shrink it before making up the mats. If you are using a patterned fabric, position the template so that the pattern appears in the centre of the mat.

you will need

- pencil and paper
- fabric
- 25g/1oz wadding (batting)
- contrast fabric
- quilter's marker pencil or quilting guide
- sewing kit

tip for quilted placemats
Use a large plate to mark the rounded ends.

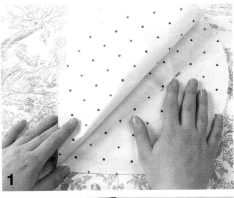

1 Make a paper template the size and shape of the mat required. The mats shown here are 30 x 40cm/12 x 16in. For each mat, cut one piece from fabric, wadding (batting) and contrast backing. Centre any fabric design.

2 Layer the three fabrics with the main fabric on top, and the contrast fabric at the bottom, both right side out, and the wadding (batting) sandwiched in between. Working with the main fabric uppermost, tack (baste) lines radiating out from the centre of the mat. Then tack straight lines across and down each mat.

3 Draw a line diagonally across the middle of the mat with a quilter's pencil. Draw further lines 3cm/1¼in apart. Stitch along the lines using a quilting foot. You can use a quilting guide to space the lines instead of marking.

4 Cut and join sufficient 4 cm/1½in-wide bias strips to fit around each mat. Turn in 7mm/⅜in along one long edge. With raw edges aligned, pin the binding around the edge of the right side of the tablemat and join the ends with a diagonal seam. Stitch in place 7cm/⅜in from the raw edge. Press to the wrong side. Slip-stitch the folded edge in place so that it hides the line of machine stitching.

beaded table runner

A table runner is simply a strip of fabric that runs along the centre of the table. Fusible bonding web is a quick way to attach simple appliqué shapes to the fabric and the beaded fringe adds the ultimate finishing touch.

calculating the fabric

Measure the length of the table, adding twice the overhang and 3cm/1¼in seam allowances. The width is a personal choice depending on the width of the table.

you will need

- **fabric**
- **organza**
- **pencil**
- **fusible bonding web**
- **beading needle**
- **large seed beads**
- **slightly larger pearl beads**
- **sewing kit**

tip for beaded table runner

Add further shapes in the middle of the runner to make a pretty table centre.

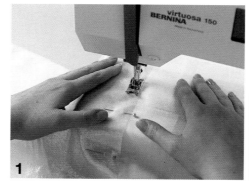

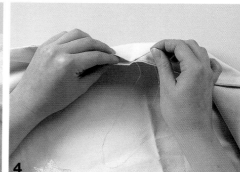

1 Cut two pieces of fabric the required length. With right sides together, pin 12cm/4½in-wide strips of organza across both short ends of one piece of fabric, 11.5cm/4¼in from each end. Stitch in place 5mm/¼in from one raw edge of the organza. Fold the organza back and press.

2 To make the appliqué shapes, draw spiral and star shapes on the paper backing of fusible bonding web. Press the webbing on to organza, using a cool iron. Cut out the shapes.

3 Peel off the backing paper and arrange the shapes on the main fabric just inside the organza borders. Press with a cool iron so that they stick to the fabric. Catch the shapes around the edges with tiny hand stitches.

4 To line the table runner, pin the two pieces of fabric right sides together, and stitch around the edge, leaving a gap for turning. Trim across the corners and turn through. Slip-stitch the gap.

5 To make the bead trim, attach a double length of thread in one corner of the table runner using several small back stitches. With a beading needle, thread 16–20 large seed beads on to the thread, followed by a slightly larger pearl bead. Pass the needle back down the seed beads only and stitch in the thread end in the table runner seam. Add matching lengths of beads equally spaced along the hem at each end of the table runner.

making a pattern for a dining chair

Dining chairs come in all shapes and sizes, but any of them can be fitted with a slipcover. The cover may be to protect the chair, to hide a chair that has seen better days, or to make your dining room look more formal. The first thing is to create a pattern, and the easiest way to do this is by "pin-fitting" a cheap fabric such as calico or curtain lining, which will follow the shape of the chair. The pattern can then be used to cut out and make one or several slipcovers.

Each chair is different, so you need to decide the style you want to create. Is the opening to be a zipper hidden in one of the seams, or do you want a more decorative opening down the back? Do you want to cover the legs, or does the chair have elegant Queen Anne feet that you wish to show? As you begin to pin-fit, it will become obvious how the fabric is going to lie and whether darts are needed for shaping. If the chair has a shaped back, a gusset will almost certainly be required to follow the curve. The advantage of using a cheap fabric for pin-fitting is that mistakes can be made and rectified before you cut the main fabric.

you will need
- **calico**
- **pencil**
- **sewing kit**

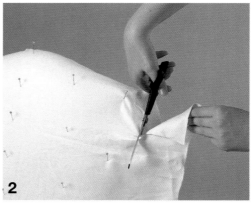

right If you are making just one slipcover, the pattern could be used as a lining for the main fabric.

1 Begin with a piece of calico at least 8cm/3in larger all round than the area you want to cover. Fit the front of the chair back first, aligning the straight grain of the fabric with the centre line of the chair. Work out from the centre to the outside edges, inserting pins every 5–8cm/2–3in, and pulling the fabric to fit snugly.

2 Once you are satisfied with the fit of the calico, trim the excess fabric, leaving approximately 2.5cm/1in seam allowance along the side edges, and the bottom edge, if you have chosen to fit the seat and chair back as two separate pieces.

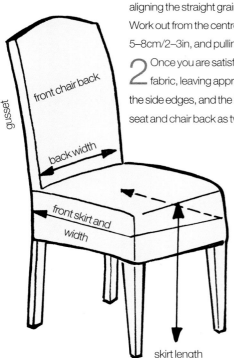

left Each dining chair is slightly different, but the terminology used is the same. The skirt length doesn't necessarily reach the floor.

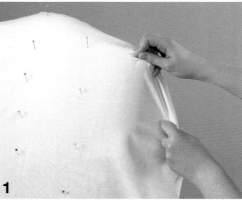

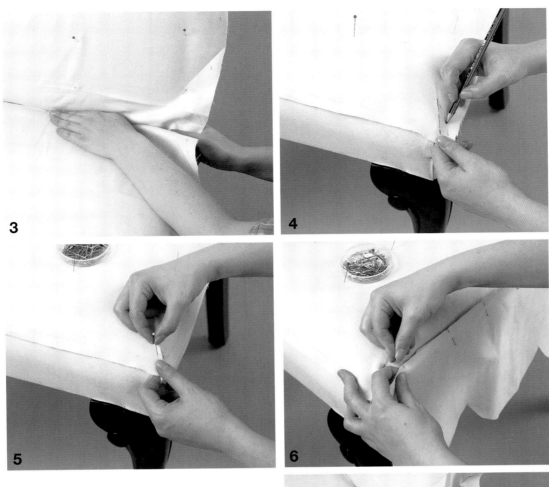

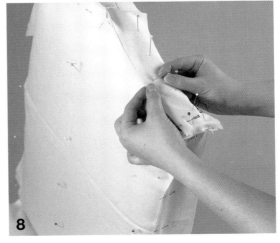

3 If there is a gap at the back of the chair, tuck the calico in. Otherwise, at the base of the front chair back pin-fit the panel to the seat piece.

4 If the front edge of the chair seat is curved, make a small dart on each corner to remove excess fabric. Mark the position lightly with a pencil.

5 Pin the darts and check the fit. You should check that the darts are equally spaced and exactly the same size before stitching the main fabric.

6 To make the skirt pattern, measure along the sides and front of the chair seat. Decide on the length of the skirt, and cut and piece lengths of calico the required width and long enough to accommodate any features. Ensure any seams will be placed at the back on a leg or will be hidden in a pleat. If you wish to have a decorative edge such as the scallop-edge illustrated, plan it carefully so that the design will finish neatly at each corner. You can use a small plate or saucer to create the curves. Pin the skirt to the seat.

7 If the chair back is quite thick, you will need a gusset panel to join the inside and outside chair back panels together. Measure the width of the gusset (the thickness of the chair back) and add 2.5cm/1in seam allowance. The gusset may be narrower at the top. Cut a strip of calico this width and pin to the chair front. Pin the seams, attaching the gusset to the top edge of the skirt. Repeat at the other side of the chair.

8 Fit another strip along the top edge of the chair (it may be possible to make the entire gusset from one piece of fabric). Finally, cut and fit the back chair back panel, which should be as long as the skirt. Ensure all seam allowances are trimmed to 2.5cm/1in before unpinning the calico. Use the pattern pieces to cut the main fabric.

pleated chair back panel

Fastened with buttons and tabs, this is a distinctive, modern finish for the back of a chair cover. Quick and easy to remove for washing, it is an ideal choice for a family home. Use toning buttons or cover them in the same fabric as the chair.

you will need

- **calico pattern**
- **washable fabric**
- **small, sharp scissors**
- **3 buttons or self-cover button kit**
- **sewing kit**

tips for pleated chair back panel

- Make a calico pattern first to ensure you understand the instructions before cutting into your fabric.
- For a different effect, attach a tie to each side of the pleat and tie into a bow.

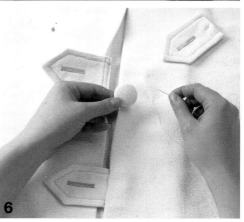

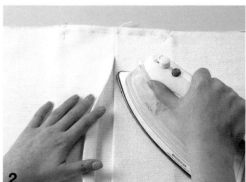

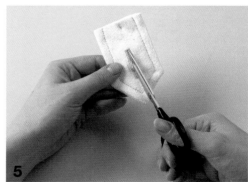

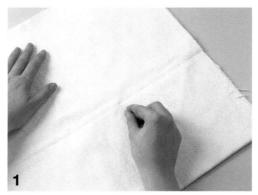

1 To make the pleat in the back panel, cut one piece of fabric 36cm/14in wider than the chair back and the same length, adding seam allowances all round. With right sides together, fold the back panel in half widthways and press. Measure 18cm/7in from the fold and tack (baste) along the 18cm/7in line. Stitch 2.5cm/1in down from the top edge, reinforcing the stitches at each end.

2 Open the pleat out so that the pressed foldline is centred behind the tacked seam. Press the pleat, then tack it in place across the top edge. Press again. Try the panel on the back of the chair and adjust to fit. Remove the tacking threads from the front of the pleat and press again.

3 Cut six tabs, each 8 x 12cm/3 x 4¾in. Cut a right-angled point at one end. Press under 1cm/½in along the short straight end of each tab. With right sides together, pin three sets of two tabs. Stitch a 1cm/½in seam around the raw edges. Trim the tab seams and cut across the corners.

4 Turn the tabs through and ease out the points. Top-stitch 5mm/¼in from the stitched edge, leaving the pressed-under edge free of stitching.

5 Mark the length of the buttonhole on each tab and stitch by machine. Cut along the centre of each buttonhole with a small pair of sharp scissors.

6 Pin the three tabs on the inside edge of the pleat, alternating them from side to side. Stitch the end of each tab securely to the inside edge only. Cover three buttons with fabric. Mark the position of each on the opposite edge to correspond with the buttonholes and stitch in place.

adding corner pleats

Corner pleats add fullness to the skirt of a slip cover and allow the person sitting in the chair to tuck their legs underneath without straining the seams. The calico pattern is extended to include the extra fabric required for the pleats before cutting the main fabric. If the fabric needs to be joined, make the seam down one of the inside edges of the pleat. Insert a zipper down one back corner seam.

above *Piping defines the chair seat, providing a clearer "fit".*

you will need

- calico pattern
- fabric
- sewing kit
- piping cord (optional)

tip for adding corner pleats
Cut the back skirt and back chair back as one continuous length for a professional finish.

1 To make the skirt pattern, measure from one back leg around the front of the chair to the other back leg. Add 60cm/24in to the total length for the pleats, and use to cut out the main fabric. Fold into three equal lengths, then press. Measure 15cm/6in in from each pressed fold and tack (baste) along the 15cm/6in line, through the two layers nearest the fold. Stitch 5cm/2in from the top edge, along the tacking line.

2 Open out the pleat so that the pressed line lies behind the stitch line. Tack along the top edge then stitch above the seamline to hold the fabric pleat. Press the pleat folds.

3 Add piping to the edge of the seat panel, if required. Pin the seat panel to the skirt, matching the centre line of each pleat to the front corners. Stitch the seam carefully, folding the skirt to the opposite side when you get to the centre seam of the pleat.

4 Attach the front of the chair back to the back edge of the seat and stitch the darts to shape the top corners or attach a gusset if required. Finally attach the back of the chair back, sandwiching piping between the two layers.

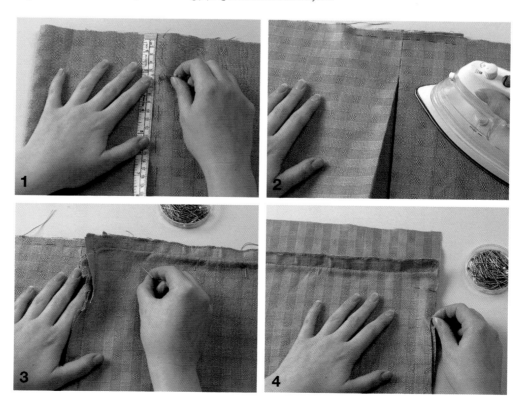

simple chair cover

This simple slipcover has darts at the top of the chair back instead of a gusset. Pin-fit calico to make a pattern, creating a seam between the seat and back. This seam continues round the edge of the chair, and is used to attach the front chair back to the back edge of the skirt. Fit a concealed zipper down one of the back seams. To fit a cover over a chair back that is wider at the top than the bottom, fit a zipper the full length of one of the back seams.

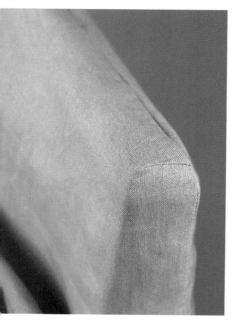

above *Darts make neat seams.*

you will need
- calico pattern
- fabric
- invisible zipper
- sewing kit

tip for simple chair cover

The skirt of this chair design is made in three pieces which have been stitched together. The back of the chair back extends down to complete the back of the skirt.

1 Cut out the fabric pieces, using the calico pattern. On the wrong side, fold and pin darts at the top corner of the front chair back. Tack (baste) in place, then check the fit on the chair.

2 Adjust the fit to ensure the fabric fits snugly over the thickness of the top of the chair. Stitch the darts in place and remove any pins or tacking stitches.

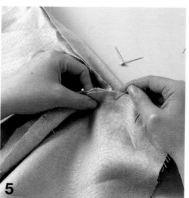 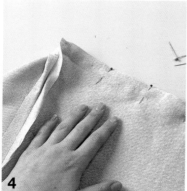 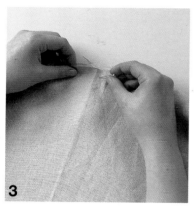 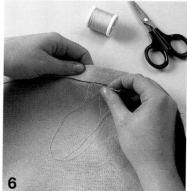

3 Pin the skirt panels together down the front seams. Stitch the seams and press open.

4 Pin the skirt around the two sides and along the front edge of the seat panel, making sure the front skirt seams are exactly on the corners. The skirt fabric will overhang the back edge of the seat panel at this stage. Stitch the seam, leaving the seam allowance free at the back edge.

5 Pin the front chair back panel to the seat panel, then on to the back edge of the skirt. This join needs to be pinned and stitched accurately, so that the three seams meet at a single point. Attach the back of the chair cover, inserting a zipper down one of the seams.

6 Fit the cover on the chair and mark the hem length. Turn up a double 2cm/¾in hem and slip-stitch.

adding a scallop edge and gusset

A gusset is the neatest way to fit a slipcover if the top edge of the chair back is shaped or curved. It is cut on the straight grain of the fabric and should be exactly the same thickness as the chair back plus seam allowances. Join the gusset at the corners of the chair back or in the centre of a curved edge, so that any pattern or nap doesn't end up upside down. Drawing round a small plate or saucer is a simple way to create an evenly scalloped edge. Plan the design so that it finishes neatly at the corners of the chair.

you will need

- **calico pattern**
- **main fabric**
- **lining fabric**
- **small plate**
- **pencil**
- **blunt tool**
- **sewing kit**

tip for adding a scallop edge and gusset

Continue the back of the chair back down to the same length as the chair skirt and cut matching scallops along the bottom edge.

1 Using the calico pattern, cut the gusset pattern pieces out of fabric so that the joins are in the least conspicuous position, and so that each gusset pattern piece matches the direction of the grain or pattern of the piece it will be joined to.

2 If the gusset panels are separate for the top and chair sides, stitch them together, beginning and finishing stitching a seam allowance' width from the raw edge of the fabric. Press the seams open.

3 Pin the gusset to the front of the chair back, matching the seams to the corners. Stitch up to the corner seam then, keeping the needle in the fabric, rotate the fabric until the next seam is lined up.

4 Attach the gusset panel to the chair back panel in the same way. Add the seat panel to the bottom of the front chair back.

5 Mark the length and width of each panel of the slipcover skirt, including the chair back, on a piece of lining. Divide the panel by the number of scallops and find a small plate to fit. Mark the shape of the scallops along the bottom edge.

6 With right sides together, stitch the skirt fabric to the lining along the pencil line. Add a lining to the skirt section of the chair back in the same way. Leave the sides and top edge open.

7 Trim the curved seam to 5mm/¼in. Notch the curved edge every 1–2cm/½–¾in. Snip into the point between each scallop.

8 Turn the skirt through and ease out the scallops with a blunt tool. Press the scalloped edge. Tack (baste), pin and stitch the skirt panels right sides together. Stitch the top edge of the skirt to the seat of the slipcover and the side edges to the chair back. Zigzag-stitch any raw edges.

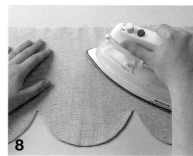

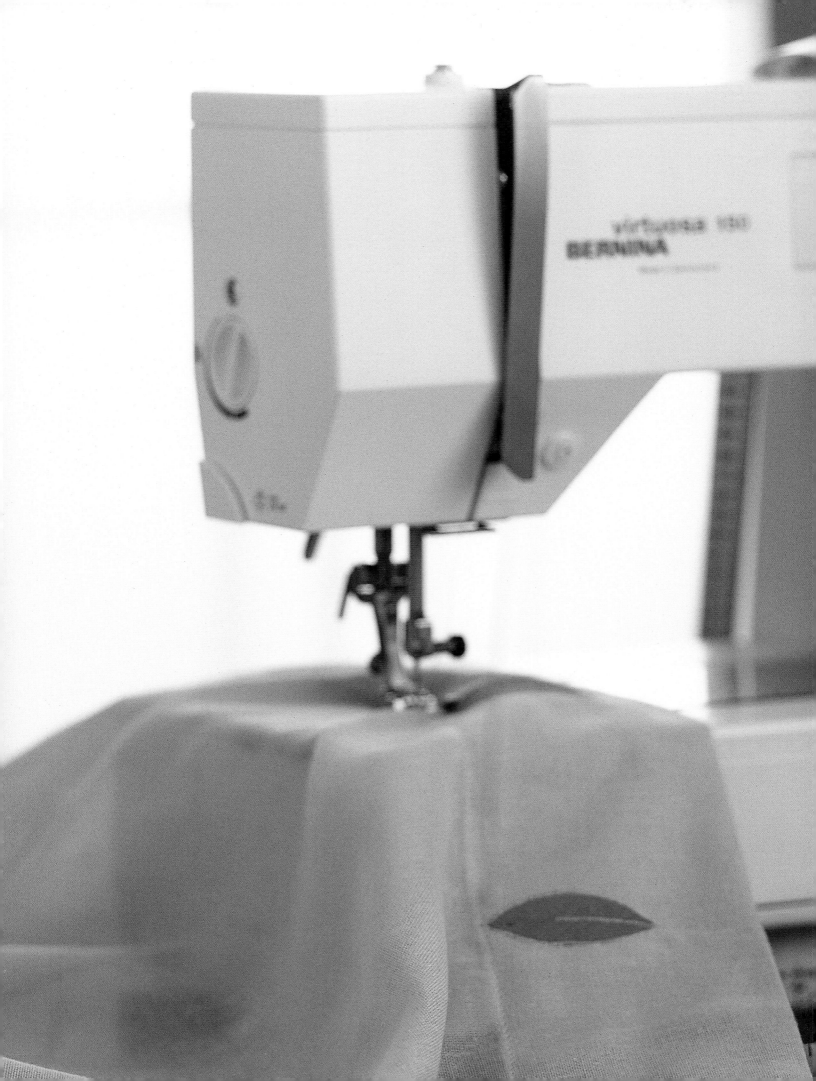

basic techniques

Technique makes the difference between something that looks average and something that looks immaculately tailored, with a crisp, professional finish. Take time to learn the basic techniques in the following pages – they will help you achieve perfect results that you can be proud of.

the sewing machine

For soft furnishings, a sturdy flat-bed sewing machine is the most suitable kind but any ordinary domestic machine can be used.

Balance wheel
This controls the sewing machine. On manual machines, turn the wheel to lower the needle.

Bobbin winder
This allows you to fill the bobbin quickly and evenly.

Foot control or knee control
This starts, stops and controls the speed at which the machine stitches.

Needle clamp
This secures the shaft of the needle into the machine.

Needle plate
The needle plate surrounds the feed teeth and has a hole for the needle.

Presser foot
This holds the fabric flat on the needle plate so that a stitch can form.

Stitch length control
Use this to alter the length of straight stitches and the density of zigzag stitch.

Stitch width control
This controls the amount the needle moves sideways. Use a suitable presser foot so that the needle doesn't break as it swings from side to side.

Thread take-up lever
This feeds the correct amount of thread from the spool down through to the needle.

Tension regulating dial
The tension dial alters the tension on the top thread.

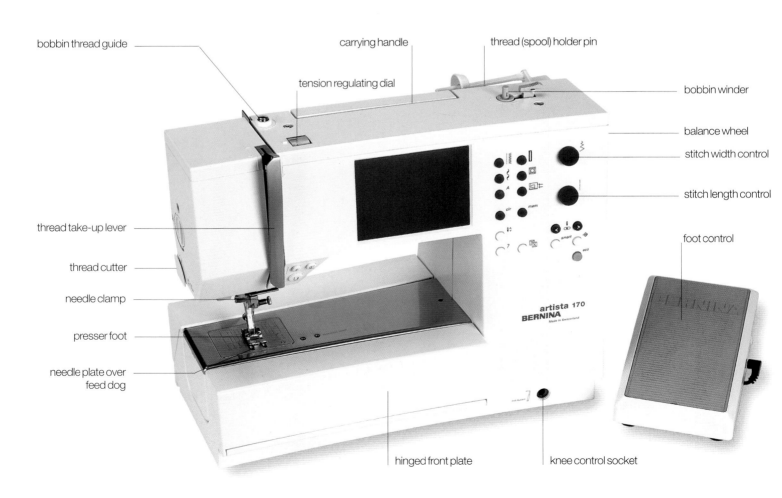

Thread cutter

This is situated at the back of the sewing machine for cutting threads.

Thread (spool) holder pin

This holds the reel (spool) of thread when filling the bobbin and stitching.

MACHINE NEEDLES

Always select a machine needle to suit the fabric and the thread you are using; this will reduce the possibility of the needle breaking.

Universal needles

Universal sewing machine needles range in size from 70/9, used for fine fabrics, to 110/18, used for heavyweight fabrics. Size 80/12 is ideal for a mediumweight fabric. Keep a selection of needles to hand and change the needle when using a different weight of fabric. A fine needle will break if the fabric is too thick, and a large needle will damage a fine fabric.

Embroidery needles

These needles have larger eyes than normal to accommodate a wide range of decorative threads (floss). Keep a separate needle for each type of thread because the thread creates a groove on the needle that will cause other threads to break.

Top-stitch and jean-point needles

Special top-stitch needles have a very large eye to accommodate a thicker thread, although top stitching can also be worked using the same thread as the main fabric. Jean-point needles have a specially elongated sharp point to stitch through heavyweight fabrics.

Fitting the needle

Machine needles can only be fitted one way as they have a flat surface down one side (the shank) and a long groove down the other side (the shaft). When the needle is inserted, this groove should line up directly with the last thread guide. When the machine is in use, the thread runs down the groove and scores a unique channel into the metal. So when you change thread, you should change your needle, too.

zipper foot   clear-view foot   general all-purpose foot   buttonhole foot

MACHINE FEET

All sewing machines have interchangeable feet for different types of sewing. These are designed for particular functions such as stitching close to a zipper or piping cord. The most common ones are illustrated here, but you can buy other specialist (specialty) feet.

General-purpose foot The basic metal general-purpose foot is used for all general straight and zigzag stitching on ordinary fabrics.

Clear-view foot Similar to the general-purpose foot, this foot allows you to see where you are stitching. It can be cut away or made from clear plastic. Use for machine quilting or appliqué.

Zipper foot This foot allows you to stitch close to the zipper teeth, and to piping cord. On some, the needle can be adjusted to sew on either side. A special zipper foot is available for invisible zippers.

Buttonhole foot This foot has a metal strip to guide rows of satin stitch forwards and backwards, leaving a tiny gap between for cutting the buttonhole.

STITCH TENSION

A new sewing machine should have the tension correctly set, with the dial at the marked centre point. Try out any stitches you intend to use on a sample of the fabric.

To check the tension, bring all the pattern and zigzag dials back to zero and set the stitch length between 2 and 3 for normal stitching. Place a folded strip of fabric on the needle plate, lower the needle into the fabric and sew a row of straight stitches. These should look exactly the same on both sides.

Altering the tension

To tighten the tension, turn the dial towards the lower numbers; to loosen it, turn towards the higher numbers. This will automatically affect the tension of the thread coming through the bobbin case. If the top tension dial is far from the centre, the spring on the bobbin case is probably wrong.

Only alter the lower tension as a last resort. Shake the thread and the bobbin case should drop a little. Turn the screw on the side of the bobbin case slightly to alter the tension. Test the stitching on a sample of fabric and alter the top tension this time until the stitches are perfect.

maintenance and trouble-shooting

A sewing machine will only run well if it is used frequently and looked after. Cleaning is essential when you change fabrics, especially from a dark to a light-coloured one. Remove the needle. Clean out the fluff (lint) along the route the top thread takes through the machine. Unscrew the needle plate and brush out any fluff from around the feed teeth. Remove the bobbin case to check that no thread is trapped.

Oil the machine following the manufacturer's instructions. Leave the machine overnight with a fabric pad beneath the foot, then wipe the needle before use. Even if you take care of your machine, problems can occur. The more common problems are listed below.

The machine works too slowly
The machine may have two speeds and may be set on slow. If it hasn't been used for a while, oil could be clogging the working parts. Run the machine without a needle for a minute to loosen all the joints. Check that the foot control is not obstructed. As a last resort, ask a dealer to check the tension belt.

No stitches form
Ensure that the bobbin is full and inserted correctly. Check that the needle is facing in the right direction and threaded from the grooved side.

The needle doesn't move
Check that the balance wheel is tight and that the bobbin winder is switched off. Thread may be trapped in the sewing hook behind the bobbin case. Remove the case and check. Rock the balance wheel backwards and forwards until the thread comes out.

The machine jams
Rock, but don't force, the balance wheel gently to loosen the threads and take the fabric out. Remove the needle, unscrew the needle plate and brush out any fluff (lint). Alternatively, check that the machine is correctly threaded and that the fabric is far enough under the presser foot when you begin stitching.

The needle bends or breaks
A needle will break if it hits the foot, bobbin case or needle plate. Check that you are using the correct foot. When using a zipper foot, a common mistake is forgetting to move the needle to the left or right for straight or zigzag-stitching. Check the bobbin case is inserted properly. Make sure the take-up lever is at its highest point before fitting. A needle that has been bent will break if it hits the needle plate. To avoid bent needles, sew slowly over pins and thick seams. A needle will bend if there is a knot in the thread, or if the fabric is pulled through the machine faster than the machine is sewing. Replace bent needles immediately.

The fabric does not feed through
This can happen when the feed teeth are lowered in the darning or machine embroidery position. Close zigzag or embroidery stitches will bunch up in the general-purpose foot, so change the foot to one that is cut away underneath to allow the stitches to feed through. Check also that the machine is correctly threaded.

The stitches are different lengths
Check whether the needle is blunt or unsuitable for the fabric and that it is inserted correctly. (Test this on a scrap of fabric before beginning the project.) Try stitching with the needle in the left or right position. On fine fabrics, put tissue paper under the presser foot.

The top thread keeps breaking
Manufacturers recommend that you change needles every time you change the type of thread. This is because each thread wears a unique groove in the needle. Check that you are using the correct thread and type of needle for the fabric. Knots or slubs in the thread or tight top tension can cause the thread to break.

The bobbin thread breaks
Check that the bobbin case is inserted correctly, has not been over-filled, and that the thread has no knots in it. Also check the bobbin case mechanism for trapped fluff (lint). Occasionally, the spring on the bobbin case is too tight for the thread and the tension screw needs to be loosened – refer to your manual for instructions.

the sewing kit

1 Bodkin

Use this tool to thread elastic, cord or ribbon easily through casings.

2 Dressmaker's carbon and tracing wheel

Use together to transfer markings to the wrong side of the fabric. Select carbon paper that is close in colour to the fabric. Use white carbon paper on white fabric.

3 Fabric markers

A pencil is suitable for marking most hard-surfaced fabrics and can be brushed off with a stiff brush. A vanishing-ink pen will wash out in water or fade. Use a tracing pen to draw a design on waxed paper and then transfer it to the fabric by ironing over it.

4 Fusible bonding web

This glue mesh is used to stick two layers of fabric together. The narrow bands are useful for hems and facings, and the wider widths are used for appliqué. The mesh is melted with the heat of an iron. Cover the ironing surface and the area where the mesh is applied with waxed paper to avoid sticking glue to the iron and the work surface.

5 Hand-sewing needles

"Sharps" (medium-length, all-purpose needles) are used for general hand sewing. For fine hand sewing, use the shorter, round-eyed "betweens". Hand-sewing needles are numbered from 1–10, with 10 being the finest.

6 Pincushion

Useful for holding pins and needles as you work. Pin-cushions are available with wrist bands for ease of use.

7 Dressmaker's pins

Use household pins for most sewing, and lace pins for delicate fabrics. Glass-headed pins are easy to see.

8 Quilter's tape

Use to mark very accurate seam allowances. The tape is 5mm/¼in wide.

9 Rouleau turner

A metal tool used to turn through rouleau loops.

10 Safety pins

Use to hold thick layers of fabric together.

11 Scissors

You will need a large pair of drop-handle (bent-handle) scissors for cutting out fabric, a medium pair for trimming seams or cutting small pieces of fabric, and a small pair of sharp, pointed embroidery scissors for cutting threads and snipping into curves. Never cut paper with sewing scissors as it dulls the blade.

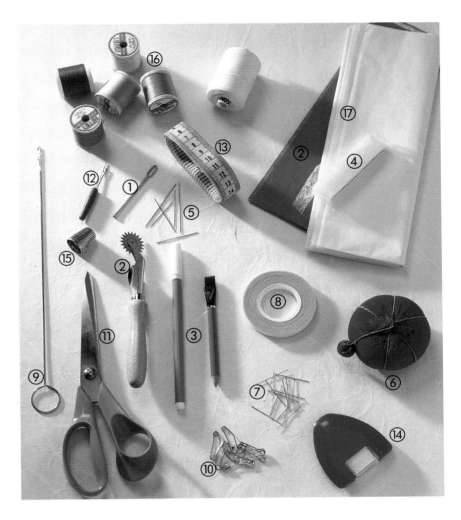

12 Seam ripper

A small cutting tool for undoing machine-stitching mistakes. Also useful for cutting buttonholes.

13 Tape measure

Buy a 150cm/60in tape with metal tips in a material such as fibreglass that will not stretch.

14 Tailor's chalk

Use to mark patterns or designs on fabric. Test first to ensure it will brush off fabric.

15 Thimble

Wear to prevent needle pricks when hand sewing.

16 Sewing threads

Choose a thread that matches the fibre content of the fabric. Use a shade of thread that matches the fabric. If there is no match go one shade darker. Tacking (basting) thread is cheaper and poorer-quality.

17 Tissue paper

When machine stitching delicate fabrics, tack (baste) strips of tissue paper to each side of the seam and stitch as normal. Tear the tissue paper off afterwards.

choosing fabrics

If one of your soft furnishing projects isn't successful, it could be your choice of fabric or the way you handled it that lets it down. With such a wonderful range of fabrics on the market, there is no need for "hand-made" to mean a cheaper alternative or second-best. Staff in most fabric shops will be pleased to pass on their knowledge about choosing the best fabric for a particular purpose.

PREPARING FABRIC

Once you have chosen the fabric, the temptation is to start cutting straight away. Curb your enthusiasm, however – a little time spent preparing the fabric before you begin will help prevent costly mistakes later.

Before beginning any soft furnishing project, the first thing to do is to straighten the fabric. When fabric is wrapped around a large bolt or roll, it can be pulled slightly out of shape and this may not become obvious until you have already started sewing. Problems such as the pattern not matching, cushion covers that aren't square, curtains not hanging straight, or a swag draping incorrectly can all be caused by the fabric being slightly off-grain.

To check whether the fabric is straight or off-grain, first straighten the ends, either by tearing the fabric or by pulling a thread (see below), then fold it in half lengthways with the selvages together to see if the two crossways ends meet squarely. Sometimes it isn't obvious that the fabric is not straight because the bolt was used as a guide for cutting in the store, which can make the end look straight. Always check it anyway – it will help to ensure perfect results.

left *Always choose fabrics that are suitable for the job in hand.*

STRAIGHTENING FABRIC ENDS

If the fabric has an obvious weave, or a woven pattern such as a check, it can easily be cut along the grain to ensure it is straight. In most cases, however, you will have to tear or cut along a thread to guarantee a straight line.

Tearing is the quickest way to straighten a fabric end but this is only suitable for plain-weave fabrics such as calico or poplin. Try a test piece first to ensure that tearing the fabric won't harm it, or cause it to tear lengthways. The safest way to straighten the end is by pulling a thread. This takes longer, but is worth it.

1 Look carefully at the weave of the fabric and snip into the selvage next to where the first thread goes straight across. Pull one of the crossways threads until the fabric gathers up.

2 Ease the gathers gently along the thread as far as possible, then cut carefully along this line. Continue this process until you have cut right across the fabric.

STRAIGHTENING THE GRAIN

Once the end of the fabric is straight, you will be able to check if the fabric is off-grain. There are two ways to do this. You can either lay the fabric flat on a square table or fold it in half lengthways with the selvages together. In both cases, the ends should be square. If the corners don't match, the fabric needs to be straightened before you can begin cutting and sewing. If it is only slightly off-grain it can be steam-pressed into shape, but misshapen fabric must be pulled back into shape. This can be quite hard work for a large piece of fabric, and you may need to enlist the help of a friend to pull from the opposite end. This step is essential and will affect the final drape of the fabric, so don't be tempted to miss this stage.

To pull the fabric back into shape, hold it firmly on each side of the narrow corners and pull your hands apart. Keep moving your hands down each side, pulling firmly until you reach the other corners. This is easier to do if two people work from opposite corners. Fold the fabric in half lengthways, right sides together. Pin the raw edges together. Place pins into the ironing board every 13cm/5in along the selvage. Press the fabric from the selvage into the fold until the weave is absolutely straight, but avoid pressing the fold. Leave the fabric to cool before removing the pins. For pressing large pieces of fabric cover a table with a blanket and sheet.

fabric terminology

It is important to understand the terms used when describing fabric. Some fabrics handle very differently if cut on the crossways grain rather than the lengthways grain, and designs can end up facing in the wrong direction. Most fabrics are cut with the right sides of the fabric together, and can be folded on the lengthways or crossways fold. Nap designs have a design or surface texture, which means that the fabric must be folded lengthways or not at all.

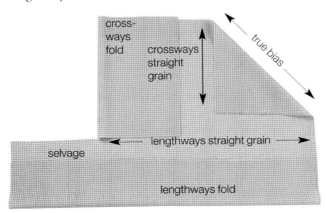

Bias

The bias is any diagonal line across woven fabric. Bias strips are used for binding or piping curved edges. Fabric cut on the bias has more stretch than fabric cut on the straight grain, and the most stretch is achieved on the true bias; this is when the selvage edge on one side is folded over to run parallel to the crossways grain.

Fold

Fabric is usually sold off a bolt or roll. On narrow widths the fabric is flat with a selvage at each edge, but on wider widths the fabric is folded in half lengthways so that the selvages lie together. This fold indicates where the centre of a large design or pattern should lie.

Grain

Woven fabrics are made up of two sets of threads. The crossways, or weft, threads go over and under the stronger warp threads which run the length of the fabric. The grain is the direction in which these threads have been woven. Warp threads running parallel to the selvage are on the lengthways grain. When the weft threads run perpendicular to the selvage, they are on the crossways grain.

Selvage

This is the narrow, flat band running lengthways down each side of the fabric. Here the threads are strong and closely woven, and provide a straight, ready-finished edge for seams such as the zipper opening in a cushion cover or sheer curtains.

making seams

Various seams are used in different soft furnishing projects, depending on whether the finished item needs to be strong, to withstand frequent washing or to be purely decorative.

FLAT SEAM

This is the basic seam used in most soft furnishing projects. The size of the seam allowance varies, but is usually 1.5cm/⅝in. Even if the seam will be trimmed, stitch a wider seam and trim it to get a stronger join.

1 Pin the two layers of fabric together, matching the raw edges carefully.

2 Tack (baste) 1.5cm/⅝ in in from the edge. If the fabric is fairly firm, it is possible to stitch across the pins without the need for tacking.

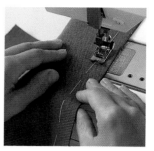

3 Stitch along one side of the tacking thread. Press the seam open. Zigzag-stitch or overcast the edges to prevent fraying.

FRENCH SEAM

A French seam is suitable for lightweight fabrics. It is used on bed linen to make strong seams that will not fray. The finished width of the seam can be narrower on fine fabrics.

1 With wrong sides together, stitch a 7mm/⅜in seam. Trim to 3mm/⅛ in.

2 Press the seam open. This makes it much easier to get the fold exactly on the edge at the next stage.

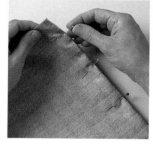

3 Fold, enclosing the raw edges, and press. Pin the seam and stitch 5mm/¼ in from the edge. Press to one side.

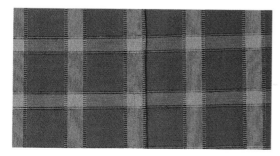

LAPPED SEAM

This seam is ideal for joining fabric that requires accurate matching as it is stitched from the right side. Plan carefully when cutting out pattern pieces in order to make the seam as inconspicuous as possible.

1 Turn under 1cm/½ in along a straight thread and press.

2 Lay the pressed edge on top of the other piece of fabric. Pin along the fold, carefully matching the design.

3 Tack (baste) the fabric if it is slippery, otherwise stitch carefully over the pins, close to the fold. For extra strength and decoration, top-stitch a further row 5mm/¼ in away.

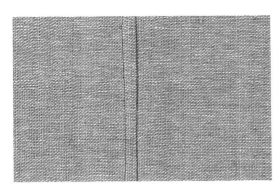

FLAT FELL SEAM

This is the traditional seam used for denim jeans. It is a strong seam that can be washed and wears well, as all the raw edges are enclosed. It is most suitable for mediumweight fabrics.

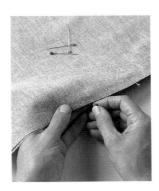

1 Pin the fabric right sides together and stitch a plain 1.5cm/⅝in seam. (For the traditional finish with two rows of stitching showing, begin with the fabric wrong sides together instead.)

2 Trim one side of the seam allowance to 3mm/⅛in. Press the wide seam allowance over the trimmed edge.

3 Turn under the edge of the larger seam allowance and pin, then tack in place. Machine stitch close to the edge of the fold.

ENCLOSED SEAMS

Seams that are enclosed (for example, inside a cushion cover) do not need to be finished, but in order to achieve a neat line when the cover is turned through they should be trimmed carefully. Bulky seams should be layered. Curved seams and corners need to be trimmed, and also snipped or notched into the seam allowance.

1 Stitch around a curved edge, using the lines on the needle plate as a guide for stitching. When you get to the corner, leave the needle in the fabric and rotate the fabric until the next seam is lined up.

2 Snip into any inward-facing points or curves to within one or two threads of the stitching. Trim the seam allowance to 5mm/¼in.

3 Cut across any outward-facing points. If the fabric is medium- or heavyweight, trim the seam allowance on either side slightly as well.

4 Notch the outward-facing curves. Cut notches closer together on tight curves, and every 2.5–5cm/1–2in on shallow curves.

5 If the seams have been stitched with multiple layers of fabric, trim them to reduce bulk. Grade the seam allowances so that the edge that is next to the right side is the largest.

preparing bias strips for binding

Piping and binding add extra style to many soft furnishings projects, giving them a truly professional look and lifting them out of the ordinary.

Piping is most often used to accentuate and define the edge of shaped objects such as chair seats and cushions. Plain white piping cord is available in various widths, ready to be covered with co-ordinating fabric or a contrast fabric. Patterned fabrics look particularly effective when one of the colours is picked out in the piping. The strips of fabric used to cover the piping cord are usually cut on the bias, but checked and striped fabrics are often cut on the straight grain to ensure that the pattern matches exactly. The covered piping cord is then sandwiched between the fabric layers of the chair seat or other item, and stitched into the seam to give a neat finish.

MAKING A BIAS STRIP

This method is suitable for small projects that require a fairly short bias strip, or where it is crucial to match a checked or striped pattern at the join.

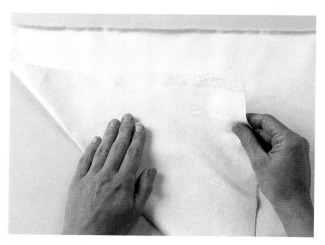

1 Fold the fabric across at 45° so that the selvage is parallel with the straight grain running across the fabric.

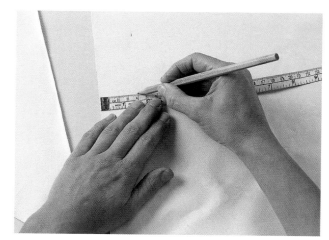

2 Press the diagonal line then open it out. Cut along this line.
Decide on the width you wish the bias strip to be, and mark lines across the fabric, using a pencil and ruler. Cut sufficient strips to complete the project.

3 Join the strips by overlapping the ends at 45°. Pin, then stitch between the small triangles of fabric.

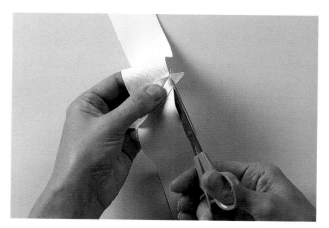

4 Press the seam open and trim off the jutting-out triangles. Join sufficient strips for the project in the same way. Steam-press the fabric to remove some of the excess stretch.

BINDING

Binding is used to cover raw edges. It can be used to finish soft furnishings such as table linen, blinds and curtains. The width of the binding can vary from 5mm/¼in to several centimetres/inches.

Single binding

Cut strips of binding fabric on the straight grain for straight edges, or on the bias if the edge is curved. Join both straight and bias strips on the diagonal.

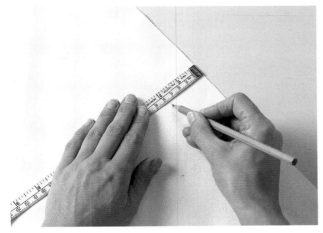

1 Cut strips of binding fabric four times the finished width, adding 3–5mm/⅛–¼in ease, depending on the thickness of the fabric.

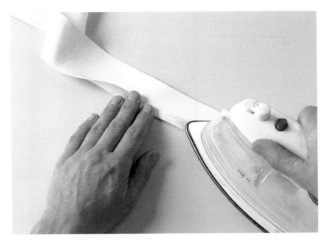

2 Fold over and press one-quarter of the width along one side of the binding. Fold the other side in, leaving a slight gap in the centre, and press.

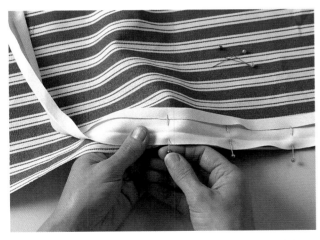

3 Open out one side of the binding and pin along the edge of the main fabric, right sides together. With deeper binding the seam allowance will be much wider than normal.

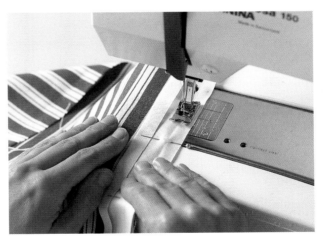

4 Stitch along the foldline, removing the pins as you reach them.

5 Fold the binding over to the reverse side and tack (baste). Hem the binding into the machine stitches. Alternatively, stitch by machine from the right side. Check that the stitching will catch the underneath edge before beginning to stitch.

hand stitching

The majority of soft furnishings are stitched by machine, but there is often also a need for some temporary or permanent hand stitching. Temporary stitches such as tacking (basting) are used to hold fabric in position before stitching and are usually removed later. Permanent stitches include hemming and hidden stitches such as lock stitch, which is used to support curtain linings and interlinings.

TACKING (BASTING)

Work small, even tacking (basting) stitches along seams to secure before stitching. Longer, uneven tacking stitches are used to stitch substantial distances, for example, when temporarily stitching a lining before lock stitching.

SLIP TACKING (BASTING)

This is worked from the right side of the fabric. Turn over and press one seam allowance. Match the pattern along the seam and pin. Work small, even tacking (basting) stitches alternatively along the fold and then into the fabric.

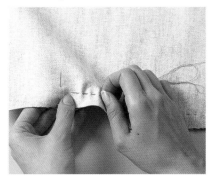

RUNNING STITCH

This stitch is so called because several stitches are "run" along the needle at one time. Keep the spaces and stitches the same size. It is used for awkward seams where there is no strain.

BACK STITCH

This strong stitch is used to complete seams that would be difficult to reach by machine. Half back stitch is similar but stronger – work it in the same way as back stitch, but taking a small stitch only halfway back to the previous stitch.

HERRINGBONE STITCH

This is often thought of as an embroidery stitch but it is also useful in soft furnishings. It can be worked in small stitches instead of hemming, or as much larger stitches to hold layers of fabric together when making curtains.

fasteners

Poppers are generally used on fitted items such as cushions, slipcovers and bed linen, which need to be removed from a fixed object for cleaning purposes.

Popper tape is most often used for duvet covers to close a wide gap along the bottom edge. It is sold by the metre in large department stores.

1 Press under a 1.5cm/⅝in turning along the edge, or for a stronger opening, make a double hem the same width as the popper (snap) tape. Peel the tape apart and pin one side to the edge of the opening.

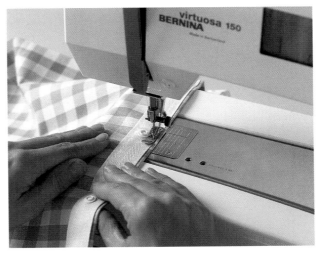

2 Stitch down both sides of the tape, using a zipper foot so that you can stitch each side of the studs. Pin the other side and check the position of the poppers (snaps) before stitching. Close the poppers and stitch across each end.

Single poppers (snaps)

Single poppers (snaps) are now available in a wide range of sizes, styles and colours to suit any fabric or item of soft furnishing. They are sold complete with a special tool and fitting instructions. Use the steps below as a pictorial guide.

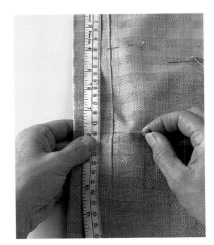

1 Fold and stitch a double hem wide enough to fit the poppers comfortably. Plan the spacing of the poppers and mark their position with pins. Insert pins in the opposite side of the opening to match.

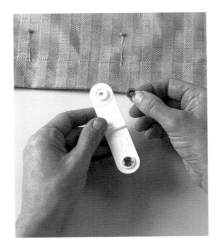

2 Sort the popper pieces into types. There are generally two parts for the top stud and two for the lower stud. Insert the correct two parts for the top into the tool.

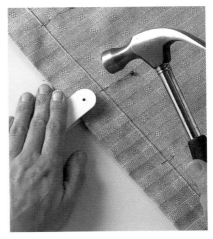

3 Place the tool over the hem, with the top of the stud next to the right side. Hold in place and hit the tool quite hard with a hammer. Fit the rest of the poppers (snaps), then fit the lower studs on the opposite side, checking that the poppers are the right way up and will fasten.

buttons and buttonholes

This traditional fastening can be purely functional or a decorative part of the item. For example, buttons at the bottom of a duvet cover can be quite plain, whereas used on an envelope opening on the front of the duvet cover they will be a decorative feature. As a rule, match the buttonhole thread to the fabric rather than the button.

MEASURING THE BUTTON

1 Measure a flat button from side to side and add 3mm/ ⅛ in ease allowance. The allowance is so that the button will fit through the buttonhole.

2 To measure a thick or shaped button, cut a thin strip of paper and wrap it around the button. Mark with a pin and open out. Add 3mm/ ⅛ in ease.

MARKING THE BUTTONHOLE

The direction of the buttonhole depends on where any strain will be applied. The button should pull to one end of the buttonhole in the direction of the strain. If the buttonhole is stitched in the wrong direction, it could open out and the button may pop out.

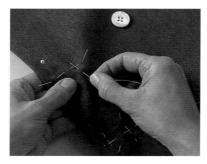

1 Mark the spacing of the buttonholes. Tack (baste) a line at each mark, along the straight grain. Mark the button length with pins, then tack. The end of the buttonhole must be at least half the length of the button away from the fold.

2 Set the sewing machine for buttonholing and fit the correct foot. Stitch the four sides of the buttonhole, changing direction exactly on the tacked lines. Finish with a few tiny straight stitches to secure the threads. Work all the buttonholes at the same time.

3 Remove the tacking thread. Cut along the centre of the buttonhole, using small pointed embroidery scissors or a seam ripper, taking care not to cut any stitches.

4 Line up the two sides of the openings and mark the position of the buttons with a pin. The button centre should be 3mm/ ⅛ in from the end of the buttonhole.

5 To make a shank, place a pin across the top of the button and stitch over the top. Remove the pin and wrap the shank with thread. Take the thread to the back and buttonhole-stitch the thread bars.

6 Covered buttons have a shank already on the underside and can be stitched straight on to the fabric.

COVERING BUTTONS

Buttons covered in the same fabric as the project look very professional. Self-covered button "blanks" are available in a range of sizes. Metal buttons are only suitable for soft furnishings that will be dry cleaned – use plastic buttons if the item will be washed. Both types of button can be used for either of the methods outlined below.

Traditional method

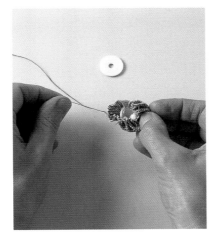

1 Trace or cut the appropriate-size circle from the back of the button kit packet. Cut the required number of circles out of fabric. If the buttons are loose, you will need to cut the circle 5–7mm/¼–⅜ in larger than the button.

2 Tie a knot in the end of the thread. Sew a line of running stitches around the edges of the fabric circle, leaving a long tail of thread. Hold the button in the centre of the circle and pull the thread up tightly.

3 Arrange the gathers evenly and tie off. Fit the back of the button over the shank and press firmly into position. If the fabric has a pattern, check it is in the right position before fitting the back.

Using a special tool

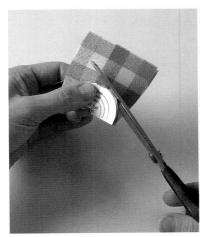

1 Cut the circle for the button the correct size. If there is a pattern, ensure that it is centred and matches all the other buttons.

2 Lay the fabric circle on top of the appropriate hole on the base of the tool. (The sizes are marked.) Push the button down into the hole, making sure the fabric edges all face into the centre.

3 Fit the back over the shank. Position the top of the tool over the base and push down firmly. Ease the completed button out of the tool.

zippers

Zippers are one of the strongest kind of fasteners and are used for many soft furnishings. A dressweight zipper should be sufficient for most soft furnishings. There are several different ways to insert a zipper, and the method you choose will depend on its position. Fitted well, a zipper should be inconspicuous.

SEMI-CONCEALED ZIPPER

This is the easiest way to fit a zipper. It is called the semi-concealed method because the zipper teeth are visible between the folds of fabric. Use it to insert a zipper in a seam, or along the gusset of a box-style cushion.

1 Position the zipper along the edge of the opening and mark each end with a pin. Stitch the seam from the pin to the edge of the fabric at both ends.

2 Sew a row of small, even tacking (basting) stitches between the stitched seams. Press the seam open.

3 Open the zipper and place the teeth on one edge along the seam. Pin and tack 3mm/⅛in from the outside edge of the teeth.

4 Close the zipper. Pin and tack the second side in the same way. Fit the zipper foot in the machine. Working from the right side, stitch just outside the tacking thread line. Begin partway down one side of the zipper.

5 At the corner leave the needle in the fabric and rotate the fabric, ready to stitch across the end of the zipper. Count the number of stitches into the centre and stitch an identical number out to the other side.

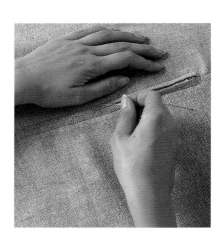

6 Remove the tacking thread from around the stitching, then snip and pull the tacking thread from the centre of the seam.

CONCEALED ZIPPER

This is a quick-and-easy way to fit a concealed zipper.

The zipper is inserted to one side of the seam so that the teeth are covered with fabric.

1 Place the pattern pieces right sides together and mark the ends of the zipper with pins. Stitch the seams from the pins to the outside edge.

2 Sew a row of small, even tacking (basting) stitches between the stitched seams. Press the seam open. Pin the zipper with the teeth in the centre of the seam. Tack 3mm/⅛in from the teeth.

3 Close the zipper and tack the other side to match. Fit the zipper foot in the machine.

4 On the right side, stitch close to the fold on the lower edge and just outside the tacks on the upper side. Remove the tacks.

FITTING A ZIPPER BEHIND PIPING CORD

This method is often used for cushions or slipcovers with piping. The zipper is tucked in behind the piping and is almost invisible.

1 Make the piping and tack (baste) on to the front panel of the item. Tack the zipper, face down, along the seam allowance.

2 Fit the zipper foot in the machine. Open the zipper and stitch 3mm/⅛in away from the zipper teeth. Stitch halfway down.

3 Lift the presser foot and close the zipper, easing the slider under the foot. Stitch the rest of the way down the zipper.

4 ◁ Pin and tack the other side of the zipper. Stitch 3mm/⅛in away from the teeth, lowering the slider as before.

5 ▷ Pin and tack the seams at each end of the zipper and stitch.

index